in

MEDICINE

Professional Careers Series

MEDICINE

TERENCE J. SACKS

THIRD EDITION

McGraw·Hill

New York   Chicago   San Francisco   Lisbon   London   Madrid   Mexico City
Milan   New Delhi   San Juan   Seoul   Singapore   Sydney   Toronto

Library of Congress Cataloging-in-Publication Data

Sacks, Terence J.
    Careers in medicine / by Terence J. Sacks.—3rd ed.
        p.   cm. — (McGraw-Hill professional careers series)
    Includes bibliographical references.
    ISBN 0-07-145874-3 (alk. paper)
    1. Medicine—Vocational guidance.   I. Title.

R690.s23   2006
610.69—dc22   2005020845

CONTENTS

CHAPTER 8

A Glimpse of the Future   89

A question of maldistribution or oversupply • Salaried jobs are on the rise • Malpractice: a growing trend • Women: a growing force in medicine • Health-care costs are booming • Cyberspace: the here and now of medicine • Corporations get into the act • So where does medicine stand?

CHAPTER 9

Conversations with Medical Professionals   99

Third-year resident in urology at a large private hospital • Veteran urologist and associate professor of urology at a large private medical school • Professor of medicine and director of clinical pharmacology • Attending anesthesiologist and director of obstetrical anesthesia • Internist and certified gerontologist • Director of admissions at a private medical school • Dean of students and chief financial officer

CHAPTER 10

The Specialties and Subspecialties   123

Allergy and immunology • Anesthesiology • Colon and rectal surgery • Dermatology • Emergency medicine • Family practice • Internal medicine • Medical genetics • Neurological surgery • Neurology/child neurology • Nuclear medicine • Obstetrics and gynecology • Ophthalmology • Orthopedic surgery • Otolaryngology • Pathology • Pediatrics • Physical medicine and rehabilitation • Plastic surgery • Preventive medicine • Psychiatry • Radiology • General surgery • Thoracic surgery • Urology

APPENDIX A

Medical Schools of the United States and Canada   151

APPENDIX B

Medical Organizations and Specialty Boards   165

APPENDIX C

Bibliography   173

PREFACE

Welcome to the exciting and ever-changing world of medicine. As you will see in the history of medicine, described in Chapter 2, there has probably been more progress made in this field in the past century than in all of the previous centuries combined. And this exciting pace continues without letup. Almost every time you pick up a paper or turn on the TV you'll hear of some important discovery being made—some formerly impenetrable disease such as AIDS or encephalitis being unlocked—new forms of treatment, new ways to diagnose disease, new medications. It goes on and on.

You are probably well acquainted with your family physician. But there are many physicians who operate largely behind the scenes in hospitals, halfway homes, surgicenters, emergency centers, and so forth. These include pathologists, who through the analysis of various tests can tell, often with uncanny accuracy, just what the medical problem is, and radiologists, who not only can see into hitherto concealed areas of the body, but many of whom, such as nuclear physicians, use radiology to treat patients.

What does it take to succeed as a physician? What personal and academic requirements must you meet? What is the procedure for getting into medical school? And how can you finance a medical school education? These and many other questions related to medicine are answered in this book.

The appendixes offer a list of U.S. and Canadian medical schools and medical organizations and specialty boards, plus suggestions for further reading about careers in medicine.

If you are interested in exploring this fascinating field and what part you might play in medicine's continuing story, *Careers in Medicine* may help you decide just where you might fit into this field.

—THE EDITORS
McGRAW-HILL

CHAPTER

1

EXPLORING THE FIELD

So you're interested in learning what's involved in being a doctor. The first thing you should know is that this is a live field. Almost every day you read in newspapers and magazines or hear on the radio or TV of new procedures, new methods of treating disease, and new drugs. Consider this: one internist who specializes in body systems and organs recalls that when he was in medical school there were only a few drugs on the market to treat high blood pressure. Today there are more than one hundred drugs available to treat blood pressure. That's good, but to the doctor, or the physician, as he or she is more properly known, it means devoting a lifetime of study to these new discoveries to keep current with what's happening in the field. Since the physician is already devoting between fifty-eight and eighty hours per week to his or her practice, he or she must then devote practically all of what little time is left to study.

A REAL-LIFE CASE HISTORY

To learn a bit about what medicine is about, let's look at some real-life situations that can confront you as a doctor. Jim Casey, a well-to-do businessman who lives in a Chicago suburb, suddenly feels an intense dull pain in his shoulder that does not let up. He calls his doctor, an internist, who specializes in the body's internal organs and systems. His doctor tells him to drop everything and report to the emergency room of the closest hospital, a few miles away. Fortunately, there is a cardiologist—a heart specialist—on duty, and after putting Jim through a battery of tests to get his vital signs—blood pressure, temperature, and pulse beat—he decides on a course of treatment. But there are many ways to proceed depending on the severity of the symptoms, Jim's previous history, and his physical health in general.

As the main doctor involved, the cardiologist, Dr. Martin, could recommend any of many ways to treat Jim's condition. For one, he would probably use cardiac catheterization, which is perhaps the key to modern heart care, and use a thin, hollow tube to handle a variety of procedures. Conditions that might have involved major surgery in the past are now treated with catheterization: a tiny incision is made, usually in the groin, and the catheter is inserted through an artery and fished up into the heart itself.

Through catheterization, Dr. Martin is able to learn a lot about Jim's heart in a short time. A harmless dye, which often feels warm to the patient, is injected through the catheter allowing the physician to determine the pressure in the heart chamber, the condition of the valves, and the locations of the blockages.

Through this procedure, Dr. Martin is able to see details of the arteries leading to the heart itself, noting blockages or placing stents, tiny mesh tubes inserted into the artery to keep the artery unclogged. These are coated with a drug that is slowly released over a period to prevent the growth of scar tissue. In so doing the physician feels that Jim is much less likely to require more operations to unclog his arteries.

Balloon angioplasty is another procedure used by cardiologists all over the country to open clogged arteries without major surgery. In this process, a small catheter with a balloon tip is inserted into the blocked artery and inflated to push the plaque (the blocking material) against the wall of the artery to keep the artery open for the flow of blood to the various parts of the body.

A new way to treat blockages of the arteries leading to the heart called *thrombolytic therapy* can also be used. A high-pressure saline is sent to the artery, which creates a vacuum breaking up the blood clot and drawing it out of the body.

Still another procedure at Dr. Martin's disposal is cardiac ablation, where special electrode catheters are placed along an abnormal electrical pathway leading to the heart and heat energy is used to destroy the pathway. The treatment is used often to help patients with irregular or dangerously rapid heartbeats.

Implantable cardiac defibrillators (ICDs) also can prolong the lives of patients with advanced heart disease. These lifesaving devices, about the size of a pager, are inserted under the skin near the left shoulder with one or two wire leads that are inserted into the heart. ICDs detect dangerous heart rhythms and in response send a shock to the heart that causes the heart to beat normally again.

These are just a few of the procedures used daily by cardiologists around the country to treat patients with heart disorders. We have not forgotten one of the most commonly used methods of treatment for patients with blockages of one or several of the arteries leading to the heart: coronary bypass surgery, used today in thousands of hospitals throughout the United States.

A friend of Jim's, Jerry Sanders, a teacher in his midfifties, has experienced shoulder pains while negotiating some of the hills for which Seattle is famous. Suspecting that something is wrong, Jerry reports to his cardiologist at a large university hospital, and he undergoes angiography, or cardiac catheterization, that reveals severe blockage of three of the arteries leading to his heart. In view of the gravity of the situation, the cardiologist works with a cardiovascular surgeon, who schedules surgery for the following Tuesday.

That morning the surgeon dominates the operating room with its brilliantly lit dome and tilting table that positions Jerry for the surgery. Several operating room nurses are standing by, including one who slips on the surgeon's gown, gloves, and mask, and the head surgical nurse, who anticipates his every move.

The residents—doctors in training for their specialty, cardiovascular (heart) surgery—watch intently as the surgeon works over Jerry. Earlier the anesthesiologist, stationed over a battery of monitoring equipment, has injected Jerry with a powerful anesthetic. In a few minutes, Jerry has lost consciousness. He lies on the table impervious to all that is happening; the anesthesiologist is monitoring all of his vital signs to make sure that Jerry is out while the surgeon and his team are doing the bypass.

First the surgeon makes a small incision over Jerry's breastbone to gain access to the heart cavity. Next, utilizing a highly ingenious machine, the surgeon performs a combination of bypass surgery and a new procedure called *transmyocardial laser vascularization*. Using a laser, the surgeon drills pencil-sized holes into the heart muscle. For patients like Jerry with advanced coronary artery disease, the procedure offers relief from pain, and combined with bypass surgery it serves to get Jerry back on the road to good health.

While the surgeon performs his critical work, the heart-lung machine takes over the entire function of the heart and lungs. Plastic tubes carry Jerry's blood from his body to the heart-lung machine, which warms or cools the blood, removes the carbon dioxide, adds oxygen, filters it, and pumps it back to Jerry's heart. When surgery is completed, the machine is disconnected and the revived heart and lungs resume their normal operations. Altogether the procedure has lasted about four and a half hours, one of several such procedures the hospital has scheduled for the day and one of an estimated 26 million operations performed in the United States each year.

We have gone into detail here because this kind of surgery illustrates the complexity and challenge of modern medicine as performed at major medical centers all over the country. We have met the surgeon, who is responsible for the entire operation, and the highly skilled team of nurses. Surgical residents, who are learning about the intricacies of cardiac surgery, and the anesthesiologist, who monitors Jerry's vital signs during the entire procedure to make sure that he is unconscious yet stable for the length of the operation, are also part of the team. Jerry's cardiologist, who by using angiography and other tests, has diagnosed Jerry's condition and called for the bypass surgery, also plays a key role.

Afterward, the surgeon and Jerry's internist (personal physician) work out a treatment plan to help assure his complete recovery. The plan includes medication, diet, exercise, and other factors.

Working pretty much behind the scenes is a radiologist, who together with the cardiologist studies the x-ray film during the angiography to determine the extent and location of the blockage. The pathologist, another medical specialist, with the help of a group of technicians, runs a series of tests on Jerry's blood samples, obtained at various stages of the hospitalization, to reveal cholesterol, triglycerides, hemoglobin, and red and white cell count readings. All of these help physicians determine what problems exist and what treatments the patient requires.

Thus we have seen how in one bypass operation, one of thousands of such procedures performed in hospitals throughout the United States and Canada, the services of a whole team of technicians, nurses, and medical residents are called on. Jerry's surgery is somewhat typical of the procedures done in the hospital, although not all are as complex or involved.

You can see from this chapter that medicine can be a highly skilled calling that involves the services of many specialists, each making his or her unique contribution to the patient's health and well-being.

SOME MAJOR CONSIDERATIONS

But that's not all that medicine has to offer—not by any means. For one there are the salaries—medicine is a very high-paying profession. According to the AMA and other medical organizations, the median salary for doctors today is $179,000 a year, one of the highest paying professions. To this many leaders of the profession respond: Yes, medicine is a high-paying profession, but when you consider the long, fifty-five to eighty-hour weeks and the high cost of medical education—$31,000 a year for state residents at private medical schools and $14,500 a year for state residents at public medical schools in 2003—it might not seem that high. Add to this the difficulty of being admitted to medical school and the problem of surviving the basic science years—referred to usually as the first two years of study, in which students are exposed to chemistry, physiology, zoology, and physics—often considered the toughest part of the curriculum, then you can see why medicine is not for the weak-minded.

Not to be discounted are the frustrations that many doctors feel with HMOs, health maintenance organizations, to which consumers are flocking in ever-increasing numbers. HMOs, and to a lesser degree preferred provider organizations (PPOs), often referred to by doctors as "cookbook medicine," create frustration by telling physicians what they may and may not do. Often HMOs cover just about all conceivable ailments, but they can be very rigid in declaring what procedures the physician may do.

Here is an example of what the doctor may face in dealing with an HMO, the government, insurance companies, and other health payers looking over his or her shoulder. On the one hand, the doctor is prevented from ordering certain tests needed to confirm a diagnosis because they aren't covered by the rules of the health-care coverage. On the other hand, the doctor may face a ruinous lawsuit for malpractice if a patient sues the doctor and can prove that an adverse medical outcome could have been prevented if the doctor had ordered a test that was not covered for a particular diagnosis. So the doctor is "damned if he does and damned if he doesn't." It has reached the point where doctors in certain high-risk specialties, such as obstetrics-gynecology, paid on average $166,000 a year for coverage in 2004. And this is just an average. Some doctors in obstetrics and gynecology, plastic surgery, neurosurgery, and other kinds of surgery pay double and even triple this amount in malpractice insurance. Where doctors practice is also a factor in what they pay for malpractice (liability) insurance. Florida is a high-cost state, as are New York, Illinois, and a few others.

If doctors are confused and frustrated by the restrictions placed on them by HMOs and various health-care payers, the public is also showing mixed emotions about doctors. In a recent survey by *Newsweek* magazine 83 percent of the patients responding rated their own doctors as doing a good job, but only 51 percent said that doctors were taking a personal interest in their patients, while 81 percent felt that doctors in general charged too much, and nearly half believed that doctors made their patients wait too long.

Another big cause of grief is the long hours involved in residency training—the years medical students, now doctors, spend in learning various specialties and subspecialties. Here the residents average a workweek of nearly eighty hours and are on call (available for duty) every third or fourth day. Not only does this make for a sleep-deprived resident, but it also can result in inferior treatment of patients as well.

And the patients themselves need to be factored into this. They often take out their frustrations and fears on the doctor, especially if the patient doesn't seem to be doing any better. Add to this the patients who call their doctors for real or imagined health problems in the middle of the night—problems that may turn out to be no more than indigestion or a backache.

THE PLUS FACTORS IN MEDICINE

Despite all of these problems and frustrations, if you can withstand these negatives, medicine has much to offer. To the doctor who succeeds in establishing a practice, whether solo, in a group, or working for an organization (the list of places where doctors work is endless), medicine can be the most gratifying of professions. And there is another treasure that doctors earn, which to many is richer and more satisfying than money, and that is the satisfaction and trust of your patients. This is just one of the many positives of the profession that more than compensate for all of the negatives.

Then, as already noted above, doctors make good money. No doubt about it. A recent survey by several leading medical organizations, including the AMA, showed that income for all doctors averaged an all-time high in 2004 of $179,000, an increase of almost 100 percent over the $89,000 that physicians averaged in 1981. Of all the specialists, surgeons earned the most, from a low of $226,000 to a high of $520,000 a year before taxes, but after all expenses were paid. At the opposite end of the scale, family physicians earned the least, averaging $161,000 a year. Salaries ranged from a low of $135,000 a year to a high of $239,000 per year.

And these are just averages. It seems safe to say that many physicians, including neurosurgeons and cardiovascular surgeons, could double and even triple the average salary for all physicians.

True, the pay is excellent, but this is offset to a great extent by the cost of education. In 2004, the Association of American Medical Colleges reported that tuition for state residents at private schools averaged $31,000 a year while that for state residents at public schools averaged $14,500 a year.

It is not surprising that the average medical school graduate finished $115,218 in debt in 2004, according to the Association of American Medical Colleges. Add to this the fact that tuition, which is by far the most expensive cost in a medical education, is far outpacing the rate of inflation, and you have a problem of enormous proportions.

Still, the medical profession has been undergoing tremendous change. To be in the forefront of all of the treatments, drugs, therapies, and life-saving procedures that have been introduced in the last thirty or forty years is a thrill as well as a challenge.

Just think of the research that has been going on in the areas of artificial hearts, heart and organ transplants, laser surgery (often used in many hospital procedures, but particularly in diabetic retinopathy), and micro-surgery to help eliminate the pain of disk problems of the spinal cord or in hip and knee replacement, to name just a few, and you will have some idea of how far the profession has advanced in recent years.

Or consider the gigantic strides the profession has made in the area of disease diagnosis—the many new tools that are commonplace in medicine today: computerized tomography (CT) scans, magnetic imaging resonance (MRI), echocardiograms, ultrasound, nuclear medicine, and many more testing procedures, all of which help to give the doctor a more thorough and realistic picture of a disease and its effect on the patient.

From this you can get a pretty good idea of the progress that has been made in recent years. One physician thinks of it this way: "If I had had just a small percentage of the treatments and medications now at my disposal to help heal patients when I was just a student, it would have made it all worthwhile."

In short, some of the advantages to a career in medicine include: you are serving people, you are an important part of your community, you are not chained to a desk, and you're in demand just about anywhere you choose to live. Medicine gives you a lot of career options. Besides those doctors whom we have already described, there are dozens of other medical specialties that you can choose from—each with its own needs and qualifications.

Doctors work in neighborhood clinics, hospitals, and schools caring for those in need. Physician researchers work to develop exciting new treatments for cancer, neurological and genetic disorders, and infectious diseases such as AIDS. Academic physicians share their skills with medical students and residents. Other M.D.s direct health and safety programs for HMOs, pharmaceutical companies, health insurance companies, and corporations.

Then too, if you like to work with people, there is scarcely anything you can do that is more gratifying. However, if research and study are your bag, you can work as a pathologist, a radiologist, or an anesthesiologist in a hospital, where patient contact is more limited and you are more involved in equipment or procedures such as the safe administration of anesthetics, much of it highly complex and calling for advanced technological skills and understanding.

The following chapters delve into additional factors to consider in starting a career in medicine. Chapter 2 examines the growth and development of the profession from earliest recorded history to the present. Chapter 3 explores what is involved in choosing a medical school and also reviews the requirements for admission to medical schools as well as medical school exams and their importance in obtaining residencies and licensure. It also discusses postgraduate training in various medical specialties and subspecialties.

Chapter 4 focuses on the factors involved in paying for a medical education, as well as aid available from the schools, the government, and from private sources. Chapter 5 identifies what is involved in selecting a specialty and reviews current methods of obtaining a residency in that specialty.

Chapter 6 looks at that other branch of medicine—osteopathy. Chapter 7 explores the various options open to you in getting started, such as working as a salaried physician, starting a solo or group practice, or joining an HMO or other managed care program.

Chapter 8 analyzes the future of medicine, while Chapter 9 reveals what various members of the profession—medical school administrators, instructors and researchers, students, residents, and practicing physicians —have to say about the profession, both good and bad. Chapter 10 examines the various specialties and subspecialties open to the student who has the background to qualify.

Three appendixes provide additional resources in handy list form. Appendix A covers "Medical Schools of the United States and Canada," Appendix B offers information on "Medical Organizations and Specialty Boards," and Appendix C, "Bibliography," provides sources for further reading.

So, there it is—a look at the good and the bad of a medical career, with no effort to minimize the negatives affecting your ability to succeed in this profession or to give the positives an undue gloss.

C H A P T E R

2

MEDICINE FROM ANCIENT TO MODERN TIMES

We have already noted that medicine is a live profession with new advances in procedures, treatments, and medications being announced almost every day. Actually, since the work of Edward Jenner, an English physician who in 1796 performed the first smallpox vaccination, the pace of advances in medicine has picked up to the point where you might say that there have been more discoveries in medicine in the past century than in all previous centuries combined.

HISTORY OF MEDICINE

Even in ancient times, people were concerned with questions of health care and treatment. To a large extent, much of this concern was associated with magic, superstition, and religion, and to a degree, this is still true in certain cultures.

As a result, medicine probably did more harm than good, even in relatively recent times. For example, during the Civil War disease took many more lives than did the actual fighting, claiming two out of three mortalities. Dysentery, scurvy, diphtheria, typhoid, and pneumonia took many thousands of lives. In one year, 995 of every thousand soldiers in the Union army contracted diarrhea and dysentery. Sanitary conditions were primitive, to say the least.

MEDICINE IN ANCIENT DAYS

Going back to ancient days, the practice of medicine was a real concern. About 3000 B.C., the ancient Egyptians are credited with developing the first systematic treatment of sickness and disease. So respected was the famous physician Imhotep that the Egyptians regarded him as the god of healing.

The next advance in medicine came with the Code of Hammurabi of Babylon, which dates back to 1727 B.C. It states, "If a physician operates on a freeman and causes the man's death or blindness, the physician's hand will be cut off." The code went on to say that if the death of a slave resulted from the physician's care, the physician would have to pay for a replacement.

In many ways, the foundation of modern medicine is attributed to the ancient Greek physician Hippocrates, who is credited with developing the code of medical ethics that is still the foundation of modern medical practice. Today all physicians in this country swear to uphold the code of medical conduct when they take the Hippocratic oath, which says in part, "I will practice my profession with conscience and dignity; the health of my patient will be my first consideration."

With the rise of the Roman empire came a steady decline in medical discoveries and commentary. It remained for the Jews and the Arabs to advance the gathering of medical information; but at the height of their power, the Romans did contribute to advancements in sanitation and the use of water aqueducts. Unfortunately, the fall of the Roman empire was accompanied by the destruction of many of the canals and waterways the Romans had built.

MEDICINE IN MEDIEVAL TIMES

The tie of medicine to the welfare of his subjects was first recognized by the Holy Roman Emperor Frederick II, who in A.D. 1240 stipulated, "The damage and suffering that occur to our subjects is due to the ignorance of physicians and must be remedied."

His solution: the enactment of a series of regulations requiring that all would-be physicians receive a medical diploma from a university following three years of study and a year of apprenticeship under an experienced physician. In addition, physicians were required to take a course in anatomy. Frederick's actions were the prototype of medical education that has guided study of medicine over the centuries.

For years during the Middle Ages little of any consequence happened in medicine. But the Renaissance of the fourteenth through the sixteenth centuries saw a revival of inquiry and emphasis on the scientific method. Anatomy and physiology and medical training began to be taught in universities, and medical training was emphasized.

A high point in the development of medicine was the work of a Belgian physician, Vesalius, who in 1543 published the first text on anatomy, thus distinguishing the *science* of medicine from the *practice*.

This was followed by the work of the Italian scientist Galileo Galilei, who in the seventeenth century first used the compound microscope to observe the human body. Later in the century the Italian physician Giovanni Battista Morgani published the first book on pathology, basing his observations on some of the primitive autopsies of the time.

It was not until the mid-eighteenth century that anyone was able to tie disease with existing unsanitary conditions and filth. And it would take yet another 150 years before scientific researchers finally understood that it was organisms attacking the body that caused disease and infection.

JENNER'S WORK IN SMALLPOX: A TURNING POINT

It was the groundbreaking work of Edward Jenner in developing the first smallpox vaccination that really dates the era of modern medicine. Jenner's work in smallpox was followed by the discoveries of Louis Pasteur, a brilliant French chemist of the nineteenth century, who discovered the process of using heat to control germs in milk that bears his name—*pasteurization*.

Several other discoveries in the nineteenth century had a profound impact on the development of medicine. First there were the discoveries of Robert Koch, a German scientist who working with Pasteur, identified specific organisms that caused several diseases. Known as the father of bacteriology, Koch was rewarded for his efforts with the Nobel prize in physiology and medicine in 1905.

This was followed by the discoveries of Ignacz Semmelweis, a Hungarian physician recognized as a pioneer in the antiseptic practice of obstetrics and for his work in diagnosing blood poisoning as the cause of disease that took the lives of many new mothers.

But it was an American dentist, William Thomas Green Morton, who is credited with the development of the modern science of anesthesiology. In 1846 Morton first demonstrated the effectiveness of ether as an anesthetic. In so doing, Morton opened up the field of medicine to a host of surgical operations that until that time were often too painful for a patient to withstand.

Next came the work of an English physician, Dr. Joseph Lister, who with the newly acquired knowledge of the role of germs in causing diseases, introduced the process of sepsis (germ control) in the control and eradication of disease. He is also credited with introducing aseptic conditions, with their emphasis on complete cleanliness, to help keep wounds free of germs.

Then, in 1895 a German physicist, William Conrad Roentgen, completed his groundbreaking work in demonstrating how a beam of electric current passed through a body could reveal internal body structure. His work paved the way for what has come to be known as the x-ray, enabling physicians to see inside the body, a process that until then could only be accomplished by surgery or autopsy.

MODERN DEVELOPMENTS

Since the turn of the nineteenth century there have been several important developments in the treatment of disease, starting with the pioneering efforts of Pierre and Marie Curie, who discovered radium, a weapon that could be used to fight cancer.

Then sulfa drugs were discovered, another vast step forward by the German scientist Gerhardt Domagk. With sulfa drugs, scientists could now treat such diseases as blood poisoning, meningitis, and venereal disease.

Penicillin, the first of the antibiotics, an immensely important weapon in the arsenal to fight disease, was gained through the work of Alexander Fleming, a Scottish bacteriologist.

A few years later, Howard W. Florey, a physiologist, showed that penicillin could fight infectious diseases. Then, in 1949, bacteriologist John Enders isolated the polio virus, thus clearing the way for the development of the first effective polio vaccine by Jonas Salk in 1954. Yet another gigantic leap forward was provided by Albert Sabin, developer of the first important oral vaccine to combat polio. Prior to the historic work of Salk and

Sabin, polio had infected and crippled thousands between 1940 and 1959, killing an estimated 26,636 according to the National Center for Health Statistics. Thanks to vaccinations against polio, only 3,190 people developed polio in 1960.

RECENT DEVELOPMENTS

More recently scientists have crossed the threshold of new frontiers of genetic research. The most important project to date is a $3 billion, fifteen-year project funded by the National Institutes of Health to map all one hundred thousand of the genes that comprise human DNA. Such research, scientists believe, can provide clues to a variety of human ills, from cancer to birth defects.

Currently, the efforts of researchers and scientists have been directed toward developing a vaccine against acquired immunodeficiency syndrome (AIDS), the latest scourge to strike people throughout the world. By 1992, the disease had killed 141,200 in the United States alone, according to the Centers for Disease Control (CDC), and the disease had been diagnosed in 218,000 others. But the CDC estimates that as many as a million Americans are infected with the virus that causes AIDS.

MEDICINE BECOMES ORGANIZED

While all of the revolutionary medical discoveries and treatments were being introduced, the profession itself was becoming increasingly structured and organized.

Prior to the founding of the United States, physicians were viewed as elite and held university degrees. Surgeons, who were considered separate from physicians, were typically apprenticed and had hospital training. Often they filled the dual role of barber-surgeons, while apothecaries prescribed, made, and sold medicine, through apprentices and sometimes within hospitals.

These distinctions did not last in colonial America. M.D.s from England were expected to perform surgery and prepare medicines when they arrived in America. And the class distinctions associated with physicians over surgeons soon disappeared.

Meanwhile the first effort to structure the profession came with the chartering of the New Jersey Medical Society in July 1766 to "form a program embracing all matters of highest concern to the profession; regulation of practice, educational standards for apprentices . . ." And by the early 1800s, the establishment of regulations, standards of practice, and certification was in the hands of medical societies.

The development of society-affiliated medical programs known as "proprietary" medical colleges followed. Such proprietary schools sprang up everywhere and drew large numbers of students because they eliminated two disliked features of university-affiliated medical schools: a long general education and a long lecture term.

THE AMA IS ESTABLISHED

In May 1846 a national convention of these society-dominated proprietary schools was held to correct numerous abuses in medical education. Initial educational standards set during this convention included the creation of a national medical education. This in turn led to the creation of the American Medical Association (AMA) the following year with Nathaniel Chapman (1780–1843) elected the association's first president.

Initial educational standards for the M.D. included the following:

- A liberal education in the arts and sciences
- Completion of an apprenticeship prior to medical school admission
- An M.D. degree that encompassed three years of study, two of which were under an acceptable practitioner

These standards were subsequently changed to require the medical schools to provide a sixteen-week course of study that included anatomy, medicine, surgery, midwifery, and chemistry. Also graduates had to be at least twenty-one years old.

Between 1802 and 1876, sixty-two medical schools were established. In 1810 there were 650 students and 100 graduates from American medical schools. By 1900 these numbers had risen to 25,000 students and 5,200 graduates, nearly all white.

Daniel Hale Williams (1856–1931) was one of the first black M.D.s. After graduating from Northwestern University medical school in 1883,

Dr. Williams helped to establish Provident Hospital, which serves Chicago's South Side. He achieved international fame by performing the world's first successful heart surgery at Provident.

Elizabeth Blackwell (1821–1920), a graduate of the Geneva College of Medicine in upstate New York, was the first woman to be granted an M.D. degree in the United States.

By 1930 nearly all medical schools required a liberal arts degree for admission and a three- to four-year curriculum in medicine and surgery. (For more about medical school admissions requirements and curriculum, see Chapter 3.)

THE DOCTOR'S TRAINING TODAY

Today a doctor's training consists not only of years of formal study, but includes postgraduate training known as a *residency*. Not only must doctors have their professional degrees—either M.D. or D.O. (doctor of osteopathy—see Chapter 6)—as well as practical training, but also they must be licensed to practice medicine. They need to be certified by a specialty board as having passed a special certifying examination before they can be classified as a specialist.

THE CHANGING NATURE OF MEDICINE

Not only has medicine witnessed all of the revolutionary changes described above, but the very nature of the profession has changed drastically as well. Today doctors are no longer generalists. Up to World War II, medicine was primarily dominated by the general practitioners, or GPs. As late as the 1950s, an estimated 80 percent of all doctors were GPs. Today it is just the opposite. Family medicine practitioners account for only about 10 percent of an estimated 736,734 physicians practicing in this country. This does not include an estimated 13,000 general practitioners. These cover a wide range of specialties and subspecialties in the profession. Of these, internists (specialists in internal medicine or body systems and organs) are the largest group, with 147,646 practitioners in 2004, followed by 79,000 in family medicine and almost 69,000 in pediatrics.

In the horse-and-buggy days preceding World War I, doctors often rode miles to go to a patient in need—to set a bone or to care for a tiny youngster with a high fever. Morris Abram, a well-known attorney and patient advocate who chaired the President's Commission for the Study of Problems of Medicine, put it this way: "Prior to 1935 doctors were therapeutic nihilists. They did not interfere unless there was something specific they could do. Most just sat around and waited until the crisis passed."

Despite the comparatively small number of medical weapons at the doctor's disposal, interestingly enough, said Abrams, there was no such thing as malpractice. "There was a lot of laying of hands rather than the laying of hands on machinery."

James Sammons, formerly executive vice president of the American Medical Association, noted that until the 1950s and 1960s medicine was almost entirely male and predominantly fee for service. "The patient was responsible for payment of services and insurance coverage was a plus."

Partnerships, group practices, and medical clinics, not to say managed health care, were all outside the traditional mode of practice, which was the solo practitioner. But today this has all changed, says Sammons. Excluding residents in training and doctors who work for the federal government, one of four physicians works for someone else—another doctor, a corporation, a group, or a hospital. What's more, says Sammons, of all physicians under thirty-six, 46 percent of the women and 47 percent of the men are "on someone else's payroll."

Nor is the profession any longer all male. AMA studies show that women now comprise an estimated 32 percent of the profession and about 43 percent of all medical school graduates according to the Association of American Medical Colleges.

THE TREND TOWARD SPECIALIZATION

Why has there been this rather recent upsurge in the number of specialists? In part this is due to the vast increase in medical knowledge and procedures that has affected the profession in the last forty or fifty years. It is almost impossible for any one physician to know anywhere near all there is to know about all facets of medicine. And as we shall see, specialization is where the higher salaries happen to be, although this is changing as shall be seen in Chapter 10.

While it is almost impossible for doctors to keep up with the entire fund of medical knowledge, it is still possible for individuals to become quite proficient in their particular specialty or subspecialty.

THE RESURGENCE OF GENERAL MEDICINE

Following a long period of decline, which saw the number of general practitioners reach an all-time low of 44,000, there has been a resurgence of interest in general or family medicine. Today, as has been noted, family medicine is the second most popular medical specialty among physicians—next to internal medicine.

Why? For one, there is an acute shortage of primary care physicians, of whom the family practitioner is foremost. Second, the government, medical schools, and almost all facets of the profession have been promoting family medicine as an all-encompassing part of the profession, in which the physician treats and diagnoses patient ills and promotes disease prevention. What's more, many students have been bothered by what they call the mechanization or dehumanization of the profession, which they consider to be a result of specialization. Also a factor in the trend toward family practice is the many students who live and wish to practice in rural areas.

And certainly working toward the increased interest in family medicine is the extreme challenge and variety of the work. As one practitioner put it, "No two days are alike. First you may see a paraplegic, followed by a mother who is nearing the end of a pregnancy. You just never know who is going to come into the office next . . . perhaps a middle-aged man with a heart condition followed by an elderly patient with diabetes or arthritis."

CHANGES IN HOW MEDICINE IS PRACTICED

Despite the increased interest in family medicine, there is no doubt that most students finishing medical school today will enter one of the more than twenty-four specialties and sixty-six subspecialties of medicine described in Chapter 10.

We know that the profession has changed a lot—that is, from the generalist to the specialist—but so has the kind of medicine being practiced. Today's physician, for example, unlike the practitioners of yesterday, considers house calls wasteful and self-defeating. He or she points to studies showing that in the time required to make one house call, a half dozen patients could be seen in the doctor's office.

Also, the equipment needed to diagnose and treat patients is almost always lacking in the patient's home. So what is the bedridden patient to do? In some communities, physicians willing to make house calls have joined together to serve bedridden patients. Typical is Dr. Tom Cornwell, medical director of HomeCare Physicians, who works with another physician and a nurse practitioner in bringing good health care to the homes of thousands of infirm and bedridden patients in the Chicago area.

Dr. Cornwell makes more than one hundred house calls a month. "I can do more in the home now than I could ten years ago in my family practice clinic," he says. "Technology is no barrier," he adds, indicating that traveling doctors can now administer the very latest in diagnostic tests and treatments.

Cornwell and an increasing number of physicians know that in the next ten years, nearly one in every three patients will be over sixty-five, almost certainly increasing the need for home care.

Then too, hospitals, under pressure from the federal government and third-party payers (mostly insurance companies), are seeking to discharge patients more quickly to cut costs.

This is almost certain to increase the need for home health care. While much of this load of bringing health care to the bedridden can be assumed by nurses, nutritionists, and other health-care workers, physicians will be needed more and more to check the patients' medical progress as they recover.

Doctors Assume Heavy Workloads

Further complicating the picture is the heavy physician workload, which reached new heights in 2004 of fifty-five to eighty hours or more per week reported for more than half of all physicians, especially those in primary care. This includes all internists, family physicians, general practitioners, pediatricians, and obstetrician-gynecologists—often the first physicians you are likely to see.

Adding to this trend toward a heavier workload for most doctors are several factors. For one, the rise in population and in life expectancy means that more people will need care. Medical advancements have eliminated many former scourges such as polio and tuberculosis. And as people are living longer, the incidence of such chronic conditions as arthritis, diabetes, heart disease, and so forth all increase, thus increasing the need for more physicians.

Then too the greater availability of health-care insurance, either government or private, has encouraged many to seek health care who might previously have done without it because of the cost. It is estimated that more than half of all doctor and hospital bills are being paid by private insurance. Fifty years ago patients themselves paid nearly 90 percent of all health and medical expenses.

Also people are being exposed to ever-increasing amounts of health information and data on new advances in medicine by the media—with many newspapers, magazines, and TV stations employing health-care specialists to report health-care advances and treatments.

All of this health-care information has made the public more likely than ever to seek medical information. And in addition, the widespread distribution of public health messages through the media has sparked additional public interest in health care.

Partly as a result of this ever-increasing demand for doctors, medical schools have increased their efforts to graduate more doctors. But in recent years the shortage of doctors seems to have abated somewhat, and many foresee a surplus of physicians in the future, especially in certain specialties.

Many Choices in Where to Practice

Doctors can now choose among many places for treating their patients. Formerly doctors were restricted to seeing patients in their offices or visiting them in their homes. Today, however, with the equipment now available, physicians have almost an unlimited number of choices as to where they can see and treat patients.

Hospitals Almost from the outset of modern medicine doctors have sent patients requiring treatment to hospitals. But today, besides admitting patients to hospitals, doctors can, in almost all hospitals, see patients in a variety of settings such as outpatient clinics for treatment of problems in such areas as obstetrics, pediatrics, orthopedics, skin disorders, gastrointestinal problems, and many others.

Just a few of the problems doctors are handling on an outpatient basis include such things as breast biopsy, hernia repair, tonsil removal, cataract removal, and many others. Even in hospitals not offering such outpatient services regularly, doctors can often see their patients in hospital emergency rooms.

The advantage to patients of outpatient treatment is that the treatment can be given often at lower cost than if they were hospitalized, and in addition, they can spend recovery time in the cheerier atmosphere of their own home.

For doctors, such outpatient services enable them to utilize the hospital's personnel and facilities—such as the laboratory, physical medicine, nuclear medicine, radiology, and rehabilitation—all close at hand and convenient.

Emergicenters More recent options available to physicians for the treatment of patients are *emergicenters*, often called *surgicenters*. Here patients with emergency problems can receive care at almost any time of the day (many are open twenty-four hours a day). The kind of treatment received is like that received in any hospital emergency room, except that these are freestanding, without any hospital attached. And often these cases could just as easily be treated in the doctor's office, except for the greater convenience such centers offer by being open longer hours than the doctor's own office.

Like the hospital emergency room, such freestanding emergicenters offer care on a drop-in basis, but at a much lower cost and usually without the long waits associated with hospital emergency rooms.

Nursing Homes In many cases, patients requiring long recovery periods from such crippling and disabling injuries as stroke, arthritis, diabetes, hip or knee fractures, or other illnesses can regain their strength in nursing homes. Most nursing homes offer care and monitoring for those who need it in such daily chores of living as eating, dressing, bathing, or going to the toilet. Long-term skilled care and medical attention are available at many nursing homes.

Hospices Hospices have been opened in recent years for the care of terminally ill or dying patients. Hospices operate on the principle that terminally ill patients should spend their remaining time in as comfortable a setting as possible. The hospice staff tries to eliminate two of the biggest fears of the terminally ill: fear of pain and of being alone.

Other Treatment Facilities In this category fall such treatment facilities as mental health centers for patients undergoing mental stress or suffering from long-term mental illness; birthing centers, which provide mothers-to-be with a place to have their babies in comfort; and rehabilitation hospitals for patients suffering from stroke or crippling and disabling injuries such as the loss of a limb.

In recent years, managed health care, discussed in Chapter 1, has come into ever greater prominence. Under this category, some groups that pay for health care are attempting to control costs by prescribing the kinds of treatment allowed. For instance, such groups might limit the kind and number of tests a physician may order based on a patient's diagnosis or symptoms. They might also limit the number of days a patient may be hospitalized for a given diagnosis.

Included in this category are health maintenance organizations or HMOs (the most common of managed care facilities); preferred provider organizations or PPOs, which offer greater choice in the physicians that you may see; and independent practitioner associations (IPAs). All three are sources of employment for physicians.

As an alternative to traditional health coverage plans, HMOs offer comprehensive coverage for subscribers. For a given amount, paid in advance, the subscriber is insured for preventive physical examinations that aim at preventing medical conditions from becoming more serious. The subscriber also is covered for major medical problems that can arise, which are often included in more traditional health-care plans as well. HMOs are sweeping the country. Some medical experts predict that HMOs will be serving one hundred million members in the very near future.

A PPO is a network of physicians designated by a given insurance company to provide medical services. In joining the network, member physicians, as well as hospitals and other health-care providers, agree to accept a lower fee than the going rate in exchange for a definite number of patients.

Some insurance carriers offer special inducements to consumers to use physicians and other health-care providers who are members of the PPO. They may, for example, offer to pay the full cost of the health care instead of only a given percentage, or they may pay a greater percentage than is paid for non-PPO providers (such as paying 90 percent for PPO providers and 70 percent for non-PPO providers), or the carrier may waive the deductible.

Unlike the doctor with a solo practice around the turn of the century, today's practitioner prefers to practice in a group, which offers certain advantages not available to the solo practitioner. Not the least of these advantages is the savings to be attained by forming such a group. For example, group members can save on certain fixed overhead costs such as rent and electricity, which are more economical for a group practice than for the solo practitioner. Also, by pooling their funds, group members pay much less per individual for furnishings and equipment and in outfitting an office or a waiting room. In addition, doctors in a group can cover for each other during vacations, and by splitting on-call weekend schedules they can enjoy more free time and time with their families.

Doctors in a group practice can also share an office manager and clerical workers to handle the seemingly endless paperwork required by the government or third-party payers in processing claims.

These are a few of the reasons for the rise in popularity of the group practice—a trend that if anything is expected to accelerate in the near future.

C H A P T E R

GETTING INTO MEDICAL SCHOOL

Okay, you've read in the preceding chapters of some of the pluses and minuses in a career in medicine. Are you ready to proceed? If so, ask yourself the following questions:

- Am I right for medical school? Do I have what it takes to succeed in medical school?
- Do I care deeply about people, their problems, and their pain?
- Am I interested in how the body functions—in how medicine can help to improve life?
- Do I enjoy learning and gaining new understanding? Am I willing to study hard and to put in the long hours needed to meet the challenge of medical school?

Also, are you interested primarily in research, clinical practice, or in teaching medicine? There is room in medicine for those who prefer any one of these areas. If your preference is for teaching or research, for instance, certain of the prestigious schools such as Cornell, Harvard, or the University of Chicago are known to graduate large numbers of students who go into teaching or research. The University of Chicago's Pritzker School of Medicine turns out the greatest percentage of students (estimated at 20 percent) who go into research or teaching or both.

Graduates of other schools, such as the University of Illinois, often prefer the clinical practice of medicine—for example internal medicine, ophthalmology, or ENT (ear, nose, and throat). Consult your college academic health adviser. He or she may be able to help in identifying schools that stress certain medical disciplines.

Regardless of what school you pick, medical school is tough, especially the first two years, known as the basic science years. Here you are introduced to the basic sciences: physiology, anatomy, biochemistry, microbiology, pharmacology, pathology, and the behavioral sciences. The clinical years (the last two years of medical school), during which you come into contact with patients in clinics, hospitals, and outpatient settings, may be more exciting but can be as grueling as the basic science years, and demand just as much study.

As noted in Chapter 1, medicine is a lifetime commitment in which you are constantly called on to study innovations in procedures, new treatments, drugs, and so forth. This is no field for prima donnas, or those who think they can get by on their charm or good looks. But if you have the brainpower and the will, you will find that the school is committed to your success and offers support of the staff and faculty that you can tap into. That explains why more than 95 percent of all medical school students earn their M.D. degree.

Consider further that medicine takes ten to sixteen years of higher education to obtain your degree: four years of undergraduate study, four years of medical school, and from two to eight years of residency, depending on the specialty that you choose. That's a good part of your life. True, some schools—thirty in all—offer combined undergraduate and medical programs that allow you to complete the entire study program in six or seven years. But these are limited programs open to only a few exceptionally well-qualified high school seniors. Also, there are other combined programs such as the M.D.-Ph.D., or M.D.-J.D., M.D.-M.P.H., M.D.-M.B.A., and finally the Medical Scientist Training Program, all of which are discussed below.

Then too all medical school graduates who wish to specialize must complete residency training. And this is a big commitment, without a doubt. Currently residents, as they are known, put in an eighty-hour workweek (and more in many cases) and must be on call (available for duty for twenty-four hours at the very least and up to thirty-six hours at a crack) every third or fourth week. Are you up to meeting the demands of such a workweek?

If you cannot truthfully answer yes to the above questions and feel that you are unprepared to meet the huge time or study commitment, then perhaps you would do well to consider some other career, or at the very least to further explore the field before reaching a final decision. You could, for instance, obtain a summer job in a hospital in your community as an orderly, working with patients or transporting them to various departments in the hospital. Any job that brings you into close contact with patients—all kinds of patients, of varying ages and with varying degrees of illness—will give you some idea of what is involved. You might also consider taking a nonpaying job as a volunteer—again transporting patients about the hospital, delivering mail, or handling various other odd jobs.

DECIDING WHICH SCHOOLS TO APPLY TO

If you are still interested in exploring medicine, that leads to the question of which of the one hundred twenty-five accredited schools in the United States and the sixteen in Canada to apply to. Here are a few questions you might want to consider:

• Is the school affiliated with a large university? This is important because many university-affiliated medical schools give preference to local or state residents.

• Do you prefer a small or a large school, small or large classes? Most of the small schools are private and in many cases are training medical students for teaching and research positions as well as medical positions. Many, if not most, of the larger schools are attached to large state universities, which are less expensive to attend than private schools. A small school may be private and independent while a large school may be a division of a large state university.

• What area of medicine does each school emphasize? While every school offers opportunities to study careers in all areas, some emphasize research or teaching (such as the Pritzker School of Medicine at the University of Chicago, as mentioned earlier), and others clinical work (like the University of Illinois at Chicago). Try to choose the schools that best fit your career goals. Consult your college academic adviser. He or she may be able to help in identifying schools that stress certain medical disciplines.

• What are my financial resources and what types of financial aid do various schools offer? If you have limited finances, you would probably do well to consider a public medical school, which is much less expensive for state residents than a private school.

Once you have gone through this list, you will have to determine how many schools to apply to. Most students apply to between ten and twenty schools. Fortunately, about 90 percent of the schools utilize a system for speeding up and simplifying the entire admissions process known as AMCAS (American Medical College Application Service).

Several schools in Texas and a few Ivy League schools do not participate in AMCAS and require that you apply directly to them for admission.

Under AMCAS all you need do is to fill out one electronic application and send it with your transcript to AMCAS (the address is listed in Appendix B). Through AMCAS you can apply to as many schools as you wish, but there is a cost of $35 per school applied to. So if you want to apply to ten schools, the total cost through AMCAS would be $350.

On top of what you pay through AMCAS, the school will send you a secondary application for which there is an additional charge anywhere from $50 to $100, so secondary applications to ten schools could cost you an additional $1,000. But fortunately it is possible to get fee waivers for AMCAS. If you prove need, you can apply to up to ten schools free of charge and pay only for applications sent to additional schools. Also, many schools also honor AMCAS and forego billing you for processing their secondary applications.

Bear in mind that the sooner you apply to AMCAS, the better. Make sure you return the AMCAS application as soon as you can. Secondary applications will be sent to you as soon as the schools get your AMCAS application. Don't keep these secondary applications too long; the sooner you return them, the better. But in so doing make sure the application is in good shape and that all of the information asked for is provided and makes sense. In other words, haste can make waste, but the slow are left behind.

MEDICAL SCHOOL REQUIREMENTS

What specifically are the medical schools looking for? While there is some variation in admission requirements for each school, there are certain requirements that all seek including a strong background in the sciences (a year in biology, two years of chemistry including organic chemistry, and a year each in physics and mathematics), plus solid communications skills, knowledge of computers, and strong credentials in the humanities and the social sciences.

Additional science courses are not required, nor are they recommended. Breadth of educational background is the key.

While not specifically required, math courses are strongly recommended, including college math and calculus. Increasingly schools are also looking for computer theory and statistics in your college courses. Also strong pluses in your transcript are honors courses and independent study or research.

Although most schools require at least three years of college work, it's a fact that 89 percent of the students admitted have their bachelor's degree and 6 percent their master's.

Note that a science major over and above the courses listed earlier will not necessarily increase your chances of being accepted, nor is it required. The Association of American Medical Colleges has found that students majoring in the humanities do just as well or better than those majoring in the sciences.

Over and above these requirements, there are two additional items that schools examine closely—your grade point average and how you scored on the MCAT (Medical School Admissions Test). Let's look at them in order. First your grade point average.

Your GPA is very important in that, as we have already established, medical school is very demanding, calling for a real willingness to study and to put in the time required, especially during the first two years—the basic science years.

Frankly, if your GPA is less than 3.0, or a B average, you will have a tough time getting into medical school. Consider that the average grade point average of students admitted during 2004 was 3.46. Of those admitted, about 53 percent had a grade point average of 3.5 on a 4.0 scale. No one ever said that medical school admission is easy.

This does not mean that you will not be admitted with a GPA of 3.0 or less—medical school admissions committees do allow for illness, financial problems, need to work, and other extenuating circumstances in reviewing your medical school qualifications, but you will have to show strong leadership ability and improved academic performance, especially in your last year or two of college.

Also given considerable consideration in evaluating your educational qualifications is how well you scored on the MCAT, now required for admission by all medical schools in both the United States and Canada. This is a standardized test that tests applicants in four primary areas: physical sciences, reading and writing ability, biological sciences, and problem solving. In 1991, in response to rapid changes in medical education, the test was revised to encourage students to broaden their studies to include the natural and social sciences and the humanities.

Although the test is offered twice yearly, in April and in August, schools prefer that you take the test in April approximately fifteen months before you graduate. Running about five hours and forty-five minutes, the test is administered by the American College Testing Program (ACT). It costs $180 to register to take the MCAT, but the schools will reduce the cost to $75 if you can prove need. To obtain the fee reduction, you need to apply months before the exam date.

A manual describing the test content is available from the ACT (see listing in Appendix B) or from most college bookstores.

One further note, the test is being computerized and implementation of the new computerized version of the test is scheduled for 2007. The written version will thus be eliminated.

Contact ACT for a registration packet listing announcements, a registration card, and information on dates, test locations, and other basic information on the test. The packet should be available from your health professions adviser, or you can write directly to the ACT.

ADDITIONAL MEDICAL SCHOOL ADMISSION REQUIREMENTS

What else can you do to help you gain medical school admission? For one, you should consider volunteering at a local hospital or clinic to gain experience in the health professions. In addition, you should strive for a well-rounded sample of extracurricular activities, both related and unrelated to medicine. These will help broaden your knowledge and development.

If money is a problem, consider enrolling in a state or public-supported medical school. These schools are required by law to show preference to state residents, and as noted above your tuition will be considerably lower than it would be if you attended a private school. Note, the lower figure for public schools applies only to state residents. If you live out of state, your tuition will run about the same as it would for private school. Remember, private school tuition is currently $31,000 for state residents as compared with public school tuition of $14,500 for residents. This is a big chunk of money, but fortunately, as you will see in Chapter 4, "Paying for Medical School," there are many sources of aid available from individuals, corporations, agencies, and government in the form of scholarships and grants, as well as from the school itself.

At any rate, don't let financial need stop you from applying to the best medical schools you can find. Often the small private school can offer a package of loans, scholarships, and grants that is better than that available from a state school. True, if finances are a real problem, you might be better off applying to the school with the lowest tuition, but it won't do any harm to apply to the small private school as well to see what kind of financial support it has to offer.

Also, you are encouraged to research the wide variety of specialties available in medicine and to discuss the nature and demands of medicine with your premedical advisor or health professional. This is the time to have all of your questions about medical school admission answered before embarking on the application process.

If you have good grades, score high on the MCAT, and have all of the academic requirements, what are your chances for being accepted in medical school? The answer: they are fairly good; about 50/50, which is a lot better than it was in former years. In 1994, for instance, your chances of being admitted were only about 33 percent. True, some of the top schools in the country may receive thousands of applications for perhaps a hundred or so openings. But this is not as bad as it sounds, for it does not take into account that today's student applies on the average to twelve schools. On this basis then, the 4,200 applications received by the school of your choice may translate to only 350 bona fide applications. Currently, there are a total of 16,638 students enrolled in medical school, about 50 percent of the total number of applicants.

Interestingly, the number of women admitted in 2004 equaled that of men. This was also the second year in a row that women applicants equaled and even slightly exceeded the number of men applying.

The increase in female applicants helped to raise the total number of applicants 2.7 percent from 2003. The number of applicants peaked at

46,965 in 1996 before dropping for the next six years to a low of 33,625 in 2002. But by 2004 the pool of 35,727 was the second year in a row that the number of applicants had risen.

Also encouraging was the number of underrepresented minorities entering medical school, which saw an upswing of 2.5 percent in black applicants in 2004 compared with the year preceding and an increase in Hispanic applicants of almost 8 percent over the year preceding. Even so, the figure for blacks enrolled showed a decline over the number of blacks enrolled in 1994, which stood at 1,427.

Also, there are nearly 3,000 students belonging to underrepresented minorities in medical school including blacks, Hispanics, international, Native American, and Native Hawaiian and Pacific Islander students. And the Association of American Medical Colleges (AAMC) is redoubling its efforts to increase the number of minorities, especially blacks and Hispanics, enrolled in medical school. Besides intensifying its efforts to recruit minority students, the AAMC is going all out to help minority students with financial and study problems to make the leap from college to medical school.

WHAT MEDICAL SCHOOLS LOOK FOR

As to what do admissions committees look at in evaluating your medical school credentials, for one they are very interested in your motivation for selecting medicine as a career or for choosing this particular school. Are you truly interested in serving others, or are you interested in medicine for the wrong reasons—because it will provide you with a nice income or because your mother or father was a doctor, for instance.

To help evaluate your motivation and chances for success in medical school, the admissions committee will rely on several other sources of information: letters of recommendation; your personal statement, called for in nearly all applications; and a personal interview. Let's look at each of these a little more closely.

First, letters of recommendation. Usually the premed committee or admissions committee at your school of interest will ask that you provide four letters of recommendation from faculty, or anyone else that knows your ability or what you have done in college. Two recommendations should be from science professors, not necessarily those who taught your premed courses.

Since many of your professors may not remember you (hundreds of students may pass through their classes every year), be prepared. Show them your résumé or curriculum vitae (CV) listing all honors, interests, and other relevant information and a letter outlining why you want to go to medical school and what your interests may be.

It is never too early to ask for recommendations, even if you are only a freshman or a sophomore. But if the professor shows any reluctance to write a letter of recommendation, back off. A bad letter is worse than no letter at all.

Through your personal statement, almost always asked for in your medical school application, the committee wants to learn not only about your motivation in studying medicine, but about your extracurricular activities and academic achievements as well. Keep in mind that the school is not necessarily looking for students with top grades in all their premedical subjects, but little else to show for their efforts. They would much prefer that you be a good student, one who is well-rounded with outside activities such as sports, music, or journalism and other extracurricular interests, or who is active in student government and other student activities.

THE ALL-IMPORTANT PERSONAL INTERVIEW

If the committee is satisfied with your credentials—MCAT score, grade point average, letters of recommendation, and personal statement, among others, chances are that they will call you in for a personal interview. We cannot exaggerate the importance of this interview, because here the committee wants to judge just how sincere you are in your motivation to study medicine. Are you willing to make the commitment to the hours and effort that are involved in obtaining your M.D.?

Since the interview is so important you need to show yourself at your best. Your shoes should be shined, and you should wear a conservative suit, preferably in blue or gray. This holds true for men or women. The interview is not the time for showing off your sense of style or wearing loud or distracting clothing. Your answers to the questions, not your stylishness, are what count here.

Besides evaluating your sincerity and motivation in studying medicine, the committee may very well want to check your judgment and your knowledge of certain moral and ethical questions confronting doctors today. Included could be such questions as these: Do you think health care should be rationed? How would you respond to a terminally ill patient seeking help with suicide? Would you ever lie to a patient? These are but a few of the questions being debated in medicine today, and you may be asked to take a stance on one or more of these issues. That's fine, if you can. But even if you are not sure of where you stand, you should be able to show some familiarity with the various sides of the issues.

For example, what would you say to parents who face financial ruin in trying to save the life of a child who is born with some debilitating disorder such as muscular dystrophy? Or is it better to try to prolong the life of a cancer patient in her seventies and in general in a very weakened and debilitated condition, or would it be better to just let her live out her life in whatever time is allotted naturally.

Such questions are the heart and soul of medicine, and how you answer them could make a real difference in the lives of your patients and their families. Then too the committee might want to know how well you could withstand the stress of dealing with patients who are wracked with pain or who are terminally ill. This too is part of medicine.

For now, you might type the key words "Preparing for the Medical School Admission Interview" into a search engine's search box on the Internet. The listings that appear will go into detail on the issues involved in many questions that conceivably could be asked during the interview.

How discreet are you? The committee may well want to know how you answer this question, for often patients will confide their deepest and most personal secrets regarding their families, jobs, sexual hang-ups, or problems with children, elderly parents, and so forth. Can you handle such information with tact and discretion?

This is just a sampling of the questions that you may face in the interview. If uncertain of the answers, it's better to be truthful about it than to rely on guesswork and come up with the wrong answers. After all, nobody has an answer to everything that might be asked.

One thing further, if you are thinking of checking out several schools in a certain area such as on the West Coast, often the medical schools will try to make it easier for you by grouping interviews at your convenience and thus avoiding the necessity of making multiple trips, thus saving you a lot of time and money.

INTEGRATING THE BASIC SCIENCE YEARS: A PROBLEM

Before leaving this chapter it should be noted that the problem of how to integrate the so-called basic science years with the actual practice of medicine is nothing new. In recent years, more and more schools have been wrestling with the problem to try to expose students to working with patients earlier in their education. More and more schools are emphasizing the need for problem solving and downplaying the rote memorization of facts.

Recently the Dean of Harvard Medical School wrote, "I doubt if I can remember as much as 10 percent of the facts I memorized to get me through medical school; we all felt that we learned more in our first month on the job as house officers than we had done in the previous five years."

It should be noted that Harvard, through its New Pathway program, introduces medical school students to the clinics and hospitals during their basic science years. Other schools have followed along similar lines, and some may introduce even more radical changes along these lines.

Typical of how medical schools are coping with the problem of integrating the basic science years into the clinical years is the approach of Wright State University School of Medicine in Dayton, Ohio. Wright State broke out of the mold more than twenty years ago when it pioneered its Introduction to Clinical Medicine course, and more recently it launched a highly successful interdisciplinary course in neuroscience combining elements of anatomy, physiology, neurology, and psychiatry for first-year students. The new curriculum moves further toward integration, rather than separation, of basic and clinical sciences.

Not all of the experimentation deals only with improving the curriculum to make it more meaningful. During the early 1990s, for instance, UCLA's medical school pioneered a program aimed at making students more compassionate. Lack of training to help develop the quality of compassion in medical students is a criticism often encountered in surveying medical education. UCLA's program features visits to drug rehabilitation centers and juvenile jails and involves student interaction with actors playing the part of patients.

Despite all of this experimentation, the fact remains that change has been slow. Schools may vary on the medical program for the first two years, but almost always the basic sciences—anatomy, biochemistry, physiology, microbiology, pharmacology, and behavioral sciences—are stressed. The courses may be taught independently by department or on a team basis featuring faculty from both the basic science and clinical departments. But in almost all schools, clinical problems or working with patients comes early on. In the first year, for instance, students learn how to interview and examine patients. In some schools, students may receive their first clinical contact through faculty discussions of real patients.

CLINICAL YEARS: A CHANCE TO STUDY PATIENTS

In the so-called clinical years, students study patients in various clinical settings—usually in the hospital. Here the emphasis is on establishing good doctor-patient relationships and learning how to conduct a medical examination, take a patient history, and recognize the more common disease symptoms.

Here too the student begins rotations (of usually three to twelve weeks' duration) in several primary areas of medicine: obstetrics and gynecology, internal medicine, pediatrics, psychiatry, and surgery.

Quite often students are assigned the job of working up data on a given number of patients per week and presenting their findings to the faculty. They work with the residents as well as doctors in this phase of their studies.

Then, in their last year of medical school, students are often allowed to take electives in the various specialties and subspecialties and in alternative methods of training—in community clinics or the emergency room, for instance. Some students work directly under the tutelage of a senior staff physician; others do laboratory work.

Often through the contacts they make during their clinical years and their exposure to various specialties and subspecialties, students decide what area of medicine they want to specialize in.

In all schools some kind of comprehensive exam is required to see how well the students have integrated medical knowledge and practice. That exam is the USMLE (United States Medical Licensing Examination), a three-step examination required for licensure and quite often for graduation. Step 1 evaluates students' understanding of basic science principles and is given in most schools at the end of the basic science years. Step 2 assesses students' medical knowledge and ability to integrate such knowledge into clinical practice and is required of many schools in order to graduate. Step 3, given after graduation, evaluates the ability of the graduate to apply what he or she has learned in medical school. (See Chapter 5 for a more detailed discussion of the USMLE.)

ALTERNATIVE MEDICAL PROGRAMS

Before leaving this area of medicine, it's important to discuss some of the alternative medical programs offered in many medical schools. As noted previously, there are combined programs linking the bachelor's degree with the M.D. Usually they take six or seven years. A list of the thirty schools offering this combined degree can be obtained from the Association of American Medical Colleges (AAMC) (see Appendix B).

Then too most schools are open to allowing students to work on research programs. Such programs, of from several months to a year long, often can be arranged to help students utilize their creative abilities for biomedical research.

For many years the biomedical science community has recognized the need for investigators trained in both the basic sciences and clinical research. That is the primary reason that the National Institute of General Medical Sciences established in 1964 the Medical Scientist Training Program (MSTP). This program encourages the training of students with outstanding credentials in biomedical research and academic medicine. Graduates receive the combined M.D.-Ph.D. degree, and the majority follow careers in basic biomedical or clinical research. About 170 openings for new students are available nationwide in this highly competitive program each year. Trainee support through the MSTP program includes a stipend, tuition allowance, and modest sums for travel, equipment, and supplies. For further information, apply to:

Medical Scientist Training Program
National Institute of General Medical Sciences
45 Center Drive MSC 6200
Bethesda, MD 20892-6200

Most medical schools also offer the option to obtain both the M.D. and Ph.D. degree in less time than it would take to obtain each individually. In addition, a small but growing number of medical schools offer an option to obtain a law degree with the medical degree (M.D.-J.D. degree). Also, many medical schools offer a combined M.D.-M.P.H. (master of public health degree) if you choose to focus on medicine and world health problems. And finally there is the M.D.-M.B.A. program for those interested in such careers as hospital director and other managerial posts. For information on any of these combined medical degree programs check the *Medical School Admission Requirements* directory available from the Association of American Medical Colleges (see Appendix B).

CANADIAN MEDICAL SCHOOL REQUIREMENTS

Like American medical schools, minimal requirements for admission to the sixteen Canadian medical schools include at least three full years of college. Included in the subjects you must take are courses in introductory biology, inorganic and organic chemistry, and introductory physiology. In general, a good mixture of the sciences and humanities (philosophy, sociology, and languages) is recommended. The grade point minimum is 80 percent plus in Canadian terminology. Like American schools, Canadian schools are looking for applicants who are well-rounded—which may include volunteering for work in hospitals and clinics, be it bringing patients meals or coordinating playtime for younger patients. These are all taken into account. Canadian admissions committees, like their American counterparts, are also interested in applicants who engage in extracurricular activities—sports, music, drama, and so forth. Canadian schools also require that you get a passing score on the MCAT. For further information on requirements and programs of Canadian medical schools, contact the Association of Faculties of Medicine in Canada (see Appendix B) or write to the school directly (see Appendix A).

C H A P T E R

4

PAYING FOR MEDICAL SCHOOL

Okay, you've sent out applications to perhaps a dozen or so medical schools, been accepted by one or two, selected the school you prefer to attend, and are ready to get started with your studies—right? Not quite. One major obstacle remains, and that's how you expect to pay the medical school bill, which as we have seen, is a big one.

As noted previously, medical school tuition and fees averaged $31,000 in 2004 for state residents in private schools and $14,500 in public schools (a lot more if you live out of state). And the average amount of medical school indebtedness was more than $115,000 in 2004. These are powerful figures indeed. The good news is that the school will help you to get through the maze of loans and other financial support available. In many cases, you can work directly with the school on loan arrangements.

Financing medical school education is something that is being done daily, and there is no reason to believe that it will be otherwise with you. If you have the brainpower and the academic credentials, funds will be available to pay for medical school and you can count on it.

But it may mean doing with a lot less on your part, such as sharing a room with several others in a dormitory instead of having your own apartment. Your school will help, to be sure, but before dipping into the school's limited resources, the school's financial officer will want to make sure that you have done all you can to tap your own personal funds.

TRIMMING EXPENSES COMES FIRST

For instance, you might consider living at home (if you are enrolled in a local medical school). This is one good way to trim expenses. But could living at home create conflicts, requests for household assistance, and so forth that you wouldn't encounter if you lived elsewhere? How about commuting time that you might face traveling from home to school and back? Long-distance travel in traffic can be very time-consuming, and your time is very valuable when you're a medical student.

And that's just scratching the surface. How about living in a dormitory, as has been suggested? Is this cheaper than living at home? Do most medical students at the school live off campus? How safe is off-campus housing? If you live in a cold climate, are heating and electricity included in your rent? Besides housing, you must also consider transportation, food, and personal expenses. These are just a few questions you should consider before deciding on which medical school to attend.

Consider, for example, that the government will not allow you to purchase a car with federal funds. Furthermore, a low-cost car is a possibility only if the school's financial officer decides that you need such a vehicle to get to clinical training facilities. Here are some other ways that you can cut costs:

- Buy used books, instruments, and lab coats.
- Buy food through co-ops.
- Share an apartment and rides.
- Work, if you can, while in medical school. This may not be possible, but some jobs, such as a graduate assistantship, can be handled during your off hours and will help pay the bills.
- Check out opportunities to house-sit, babysit, or pet-sit.
- Put any talents you have in such areas as flower arranging, singing, or playing an instrument into a part-time job for some extra income.

THE SCHOOL'S FINANCIAL AID PACKAGE

On a par with trimming expenses is reviewing the financial package available from the medical school. Before deciding which school to attend, you should explore the financial packages offered by various schools you are considering. Here are a few questions you should ask:

- Does the school have an emergency loan fund? If so, how much can you borrow and how soon can you obtain a loan?
- How many students at the school are working?
- How many students have had to leave for financial reasons?
- What is the average debt of students who are enrolled at the school?
- Does the school have a loan forgiveness program for students with massive debts?

If you are lucky enough to have been accepted by several schools, a visit to your two top choices and the answers you get to the following questions will help you to make your decision.

- What resources can the school offer such as low-interest loans and scholarships? These are especially important in deciding between a public and a private school.
- If the financial package is good for the first year, will the school offer an equally attractive package in the years to follow?
- In the financial package offered, are any of the funds packaged with low-interest federal loans?
- Does the school offer merit scholarships? If so, what are the qualifications and for how many years are they in effect?

Usually, the financial package offered is a mix of loans and scholarships. Since federal loans account for about two-thirds of all student financial aid, it's important to understand the various programs and requirements of funds available through the U.S. Department of Education. A few of the major ones are described later in this chapter.

Here's something else to think about: it's a good idea to keep a tight rein on debt obligations because you never know when unexpected expenses may crop up. Although there is a good chance that you will obtain a residency that will help you pay off a part of your debt, it's quite unlikely that your salary during residency, which is when most loan repayment goes into effect, will keep pace with inflation on the year of the residencies. Usually first year residents earn around $40,000 a year.

Before we get into specific financial aid programs, remember that nearly everyone borrows money, whether for medical school, college, or a car. There is nothing wrong with borrowing as long as you maintain control of your needs and wants and know what your present and future priorities are. Monetary Decisions for Medical Doctors (M.D.s) is a computer-based program that is a good source of updated information for whatever stage of education you are in. You can find it at the Association of American Medical Colleges website (www.aamc.org).

FEDERAL AND STATE AID

The major advantage of federal loans (such as the Stafford Loans listed later in this chapter) is that they often offer better interest rates and easier repayment terms than loans available from private lenders. The federal government also offers scholarship programs for students who can prove financial need—programs that cover tuition and living expenses in exchange for a commitment to serve either with the armed forces or an underserved community. For information about federal financial aid, contact the Federal Student Aid Information Center at 1-800-433-3243.

To receive any kind of federal aid, you must submit the Free Application for Federal Student Aid (FAFSA) form. This form requests a variety of information that is used to determine financial need of the student, which is the gap between what the student can contribute to his or her education and what it will cost. Often such a need may not be completely made up by federal sources and you will have to look for other sources of aid, many of which also require that you file a FAFSA with the federal government before they will consider offering you a loan.

Quite often, for each type of federal financial aid available, there may be similar opportunities at the state level. State-sponsored loan programs or grants may depend on if you are a state resident, the location of your medical school, or your commitment to pursue a medical residency or fellowship and to practice in the state following graduation. Contact your financial aid office, state department of education, or your state medical society to see what resources are offered.

OTHER SOURCES OF AID

Besides state or federal government aids, there are many private loan and scholarship programs that offer funds to qualified medical students that should not be overlooked. Often banks and other financial institutions, as well as organizations specializing in private financing to students, offer a mixture of programs that supplement aid received through governmental sources. Then too, many unions, businesses, and ethnic or religious groups sponsor tuition assistance programs for employees or members and their families.

Don't overlook the many foundations, religious organizations, community organizations, and civic groups that offer grants to students who meet certain criteria. Check the Web to locate organizations you might want to pursue. If your parents are members of any professional, social, or religious groups, check with the administrative directors of such groups about loan or grant opportunities.

Finally, contact the American Medical Association Foundation, which supports medical education by awarding nearly $2 million annually in grants to medical schools. Most of the grants are designated for the donors' old schools. While the specific programs supported by the donations are awarded at the discretion of the medical schools, the funds must be used for student assistance. For information about funds available through the AMA Foundation Medical Assistance fund, contact the financial aid officer at your school or the dean.

Also, the chances are excellent that the medical school may have a number of private loan funds available to qualified students, and this can be a big help.

FEDERAL LOAN PROGRAMS

Federal loan programs are a major source of funds for many medical school students. Following are descriptions of these programs.

• **Stafford Loans.** Subsidized loans of up to $8,500 a year are awarded on the basis of need. The federal government pays the interest on the loan while you are in school and through the grace period. In unsubsidized Stafford Loans, not based on need, the interest accrues.

Students can borrow up to $18,500 in Stafford Loans per academic year, obtained either as direct loans through the Federal Direct Student Loan Program (FDSLP) or through loans to students in the Federal Family Education Loan Program. Contact the Federal Student Aid Information Center at 1-800-433-3243 or your financial aid office for further information.

• **Federal Perkins Loan.** This is a need-based loan program with a borrowing limit of $5,000 a year, with a total not to exceed $30,000 including undergraduate loans. You are responsible for repayment nine months after graduation. Interest does not accrue until after the grace period ends. Contact the Federal Student Aid Information Center at 1-800-433-3243.

• **Loans for Disadvantaged Students (LDS).** A comprehensive loan program designed to offer medical students access to educational funds under favorable loan terms and conditions. You must be enrolled or accepted by an AAMC member school as a full-time student. Contact the Association of American Medical Colleges at aamc.org/stuapps/finaid/medloans or customer service at 1-800-858-5050.

All of these programs vary considerably on such features as borrowing limits, interest rates, when interest accrues, when repayment begins, grace periods, deferments, and so forth. It is very important that you review each of these carefully in deciding which you will accept, assuming you have a choice.

The Stafford Loan, for instance, offering a maximum of $8,500 a year, provides the foundation for nearly all student loan programs.

PRIVATE LOAN SOURCES

Following are some good sources of private loans.

AAMC Medloans

Under the category of private loans, the AAMC Medloans program is of special interest and was designed specifically for medical students. It includes:

• The federal Stafford Loan program
• Medloans Consolidation Loan—to consolidate various loans
• Medloans Alternative Loan Program (ALP)
• Medex Loan Program for financing residency interview travel and relocation expenses

Under the Medloans program, the Student Loan Marketing Association (known as Sallie Mae) can help to reduce the cost of student loans. Now in its twentieth year, Medloans has provided more than $1.3 billion of continuous and affordable loan funds for medical students. Through the Healthier Returns program, borrowers receive a credit or cash based on 3.5 percent of the original Medloans Stafford Loan amount. In addition a credit or cash back based on 4.5 percent of the original Medloans Stafford Loan amount is offered through the Medloans Stafford Cash Back program.

Under the Medloans Alternative Loan Program (ALP) borrowers can receive additional financing at competitive rates. Medloans also offers the Medex loan that helps students in their final year of medical school to cover the costs of residency interviews and relocation. Loans carry a lifetime maximum of $220,000 (total indebtedness from all sources). ALP and Medex repayment terms are up to twenty years, with repayment starting three years from graduation.

Private lenders, usually banks, offer a variety of loans (often referred to as "alternative loans") to medical students. Usually banks are willing to offer these loans even though the loans are not guaranteed by the federal government. These are the most expensive loans available to medical students, but competition from funds, federal and state, has caused these loans to become more favorable in recent years. Private alternative loans must be certified by the financial aid officer at the medical school the borrower is attending. For more information, contact the Association of American Medical Colleges (see Appendix B).

LOAN REPAYMENT AID

There are several programs in which loans are repaid if you agree to assume certain obligations. These include the following:

• **National Health Service Corps Loan Repayment Program.** Open to physicians who have completed their residencies and agree to serve in various eligible communities. In addition to loan repayment, you receive a salary and other benefits. Online information on this program is offered on bphc.hrsa.dhhs.gov/nhsc.

• **National Institutes of Health Repayment Program.** This program will provide up to $35,000 a year to physicians who agree to conduct AIDS, clinical, or general research. Contact:

NIH Loan Repayment Program
Federal Building, Room 604
7550 Wisconsin Avenue
Bethesda, MD 20892-9121
1-800-528-7689
http://lrp.info.nih.gov

SCHOLARSHIPS: A PRIMARY SOURCE OF AID

Scholarships, a primary source of funds for more than half of all medical students, are offered through several sources: the medical schools themselves, which may have several scholarships available through the contributions of charitably minded individuals; corporations; foundations; and several federal programs. Other scholarships are limited to students of a given ethnic, religious, or racial group, or from a given community or state. There are literally hundreds of such scholarships. It might take some legwork and research to find these, but the effort may well be worthwhile.

Several federal programs offer scholarships. For information on federal scholarships, contact the Federal Student Information Center at 1-800-433-3243.

National Health Service Corps Scholarship

Recipients receive tuition, fees, books, supplies, and a monthly stipend for up to four years. You must be enrolled in an accredited allopathic (M.D.) or osteopathic medical school. For information contact:

NHSC Scholarship Program
2070 Chain Bridge Road, Suite 450
Vienna, VA 22182-2536
1-800-221-9393

Armed Forces Health Professions Scholarship Program

Provides full support for the medical student while in school in exchange for service in any branch of the military—army, navy, or air force—on graduation. Service is one year for each year of support received, plus participation in postgraduate training programs conducted at a military facility. For information contact:

Air Force Medical Recruiting Division HQ
550 D Street W., Suite 1
Randolph AFB, TX 78150-4527

U.S. Army Health Professionals Support Agency SPS-PD
5109 Leesburg Pike
Falls Church, VA 22041-3258

Commander, Navy Recruiting Command
801 North Randolph
Arlington, VA 22203-1991

Keep in mind that either through your school's resources or your own efforts, funds are available. But it won't just fall into your lap, no matter how good a student you are. It will take a little research and effort, but if you work at it, you will find the financial support that you need.

C H A P T E R
5

SELECTING A SPECIALTY AND LANDING A RESIDENCY

At this stage of your life, as you consider entering medical school, you're probably anxious to concentrate on your medical studies and ready to go. But at this point you are called on to make what might quite possibly be the most important decision of all—your choice of a specialty, a decision that could determine how satisfied you'll be with your medical career. There are plenty of these—twenty-four specialties and sixty-six subspecialties— and they are growing in number every year.

In a recent AMA survey, 25 percent of practicing physicians said that, given what they now know about medicine, they would probably not have gone to medical school; 14 percent said they would definitely have chosen another career. Added to the 1 percent who were unsure, this came to a staggering 40 percent of practicing physicians who thought they might be better off in some other career.

But before you slam the door on all thoughts of a medical career, consider that few if any careers offer the options that medicine does. For instance, if you like to find quick solutions to problems confronting your patients, you might consider surgery or urology. Of if you prefer to build lasting relationships with your patients, you could go into primary care: internal medicine, pediatrics, or ob-gyn. Or perhaps you would like more control over your hours and are technically minded, then radiology or pathology might be your best bet.

Medicine offers a wide and often bewildering array of choices for students of varying skills and needs, and it's not getting any easier. Under these circumstances, it's easy to see how you could make the wrong choice and be soured on the entire profession.

Training in each of these specialty and subspecialty areas is offered in more than a thousand institutions throughout the nation, primarily in large, acute-care hospitals. These programs are described in Chapter 10. For now, let's zero in on the issue of selecting a medical specialty.

In selecting a specialty, you should consider the various factors that reflect your interests and skills. In a recent survey, medical students indicated the following factors as most instrumental in forming their own choice: 81 percent indicated that time available for their family and personal lives was most important; 53 percent listed as a major influence the need for professional independence; 29 percent chose the personal income factor; 29 percent indicated the chance of incurring medical malpractice suits as an important factor; and 10 percent took into account the chances of contracting AIDS as yet another serious consideration. Another factor that influenced many students into selecting medical careers was "the opportunity to use special talents and abilities."

Although the opportunity to earn an adequate income is certainly a legitimate consideration, your decision should not be based solely or even primarily on the prospect of making a lot of money. For one thing, the specialties in greatest demand are changing radically. Surgery, the medical specialty that seemed to offer the biggest bucks in recent years, is reaching the saturation point, especially in such highly specialized areas as neurosurgery or cardiovascular surgery. True, there will always be a demand for those who are especially talented in these areas, but the competition in these and other areas of surgery can be expected to grow in the near future.

On the other hand, primary care, including internal medicine and family practice, which used to be on the low end of the salary totem pole, is coming on strong. Because of the demand for qualified professionals in this area, salaries are expected to zoom in years to come.

So earnings potential, though important, should not be the deciding factor in your choice of specialties. More important is your personality. You may, for instance, lack the kind of personality to make the grade in surgery, but so what—you have many other specialties and subspecialties to choose from. Rather than risk a lifetime of dissatisfaction and unhappiness, you might be better off choosing a specialty that pays a little less but is more emotionally attuned to your personality.

It's a fact that between 60 and 75 percent of all medical students change specialties during school, while 20 percent of all residents switch to other medical specialties. Even 16 percent of all practicing physicians change specialties at some time during their careers.

THE BIG QUESTION: WHICH SPECIALTY TO SELECT

Rather than risk finding yourself unhappy and perhaps miserable midway through your career, you should make it your business to choose a specialty that best seems to meet your needs and wants—one that will pay off in increased personal satisfaction and career growth.

How do you go about choosing a specialty that most closely matches your needs and personality? This is a tough question. To start with, you need to ask yourself some questions to evaluate your strengths and aptitudes as well as your interests. Do you, for instance, prefer a quick resolution to medical problems, or would you prefer to build long-term relationships with patients? In the first case you'd probably be better off with surgery, and in the second, you would probably do well in primary care.

Next, look over the various specialties listed in Chapter 10 to see which ones seem to match your personality and needs the most. Then you need to gather as much information as you can about the specialties of greatest appeal, and then through reading and actual experience confirm your first impressions or reject them based on fact and not on initial reactions of emotions.

While all of the considerations mentioned should influence what specialty you choose, let's face it, most medical students choose a specialty as a result of the round robin of clerkships they run into in their third year of medical school. For better or worse, this usually comes about halfway through the third year, after which most students are involved in the complex and often frustrating problem of finding a residency that will give them the training they need for licensure and certification as a specialist.

While the procedure has worked to both the students' and the profession's advantage, it is nevertheless often misleading, since it is based on limited exposure and choice of settings. Usually, though not always, students choose a specialty because of what they see or do in a very limited setting, or because they get a very negative (or positive) picture of a specialty due to some uncharacteristic or exaggerated experience, which can either spoil or enhance their appreciation of a given specialty.

Why do we say limited? Because, traditionally, clinical rotations in most schools are limited to such fields as internal medicine, surgery, pediatrics, neurology, obstetrics, and psychiatry. In the past, these were the specialties of greatest popularity and demand. But according to an AMA survey, in recent years some of these fields, especially surgery, have become highly competitive and may not offer the career future they once did.

HOW TO GET A HANDLE ON YOUR LIKES

So, how do you get a handle on your interests, likes, and aptitudes for a particular specialty? Perhaps a method that is as good as any is to be found in the book *How to Choose a Medical Specialty* by Anita Taylor, which should be found in your medical school library. This book describes each of the major specialties and subspecialties ranked according to the various considerations that go into making a decision, followed by a self-assessment quiz for each. After completing the quizzes, you can see where you scored best and make your choice accordingly.

A book that offers a somewhat similar self-evaluation quiz is Kenneth Iserson's *Getting into a Residency*. Iserson offers a personal trait analysis that lists forty traits you are asked to rank according to those you like, those in which you have strengths and may also like, or those in which you have no special talents or strengths. He then rates these as High Priority, Priority, Acceptable, or Reject.

While useful in matching the major specialties to your talents and interests, the book does not rank the subspecialties of each, which in some cases differ radically from the skills and aptitudes called for in the specialty. For example, cardiology, a subspecialty of internal medicine, often requires that you be able to do cardiac catheterization and other heart diagnostic tests, which differ considerably from the skills and the type of work performed by the average internist in other areas.

Other useful resources in choosing a specialty include the Glaxo Pathway Evaluation Program offered in some medical schools, which offers a self-evaluation handout, and the Myers-Briggs Type Indicator or the Medical

Specialty Preference Inventory. The latter in particular shows how your interests compare with those of physicians in the various medical specialties.

Additional information on medical specialties is available from some journals of the AMA and from the American Board of Medical Specialties (ABMS) (see Appendix B), and *New Physician* runs a yearly review of the medical specialties that is very helpful. Also, the specialty societies themselves (see Appendix B) can be of great help in supplying information on the specialty in question. And a good deal of medical specialty information can be found online at ABMS.org, the website of the ABMS. The ABMS also publishes a rundown on recognized specialties and subspecialties, *Which Medical Specialist for You*, as well as a brochure, *Medical Specialty Certification and Related Matters*, that provides information about medicine as a profession and about certification for the medical student, the resident, and others, as well as a list of sources of additional information.

OF PRIME CONSIDERATION: EARNING A GOOD SALARY

As noted above, one of the primary considerations in choosing a specialty is the ability to earn a good income. This is especially so in light of the ever-rising cost of medical practice, especially of malpractice insurance, and the very lofty medical debt with which the average student leaves medical school, which as noted in Chapter 4 is now more than $115,000, roughly a 54 percent increase over 1994, which in turn was better than a 50 percent increase in indebtedness over 1989.

Is it any wonder that the chance of making a good salary becomes a very important factor in rating the various specialties? And as has been true in the past and is still true today, though not as important a factor as in the past, the surgical specialties pay more because reimbursement schedules are still based on the concept, rightly or wrongly, that *procedural activities* (certain *doing* procedures) deserve higher payment than *cognitive procedures*, which are based more on your medical knowledge. Ordinarily, we associate cognitive skills with primary care practitioners such as the internist, pediatrician, and family or general practice doctor.

In recent years, however, several factors have come into play that may change this method of payment considerably. For one, there is the Resource-

Based Relative Value Scale (RBRVS), which Medicare and other third-party payers are relying on increasingly in reimbursement of physicians. Under this system, a combination of factors such as time spent with patients, cost of the physician's training, and cost of practice are all considered. There are winners and losers under this system, although the AMA estimates that most (about 75 percent) of practicing physicians would either gain or be unaffected. Rates paid to surgeons, pathologists, and radiologists, for instance, would most likely drop considerably, while those for family physicians, internists, and psychiatrists would rise appreciably. Even so, the present gap between the income of surgeons and that of generalists or internists would still exist.

Also expected to seriously affect physician income is the relatively recent introduction of what are known as Diagnosis-Related Groups (DRGs), in which the federal government, in such programs as Medicare and Medicaid, has established rates for most diagnoses and diseases based on the going rates of practice.

These then become the basis of rates paid to physicians and to other health-care providers including hospitals. If the physician's charges are lower than or in line with these standard rates, he or she will break even or even make money on the patients being treated. If, however, the physician encounters unanticipated problems in treating a patient or the costs are higher than anticipated, the doctor is limited to only the amount called for by the DRG.

In summary, while surgeons have traditionally been the top revenue earners in medicine, and still are to a great extent, there are indications that the entire revenue picture will change in a few years, and this could help to close the revenue gap between the various medical specialties.

AN IMPORTANT CONSIDERATION: DEMAND

One other factor that must be taken into account is the anticipated demand for various medical specialists in the future. And here the picture is somewhat muddled, to put it mildly.

There are those, for instance, who believe that within the next fifteen to twenty years there will be a serious shortage of practitioners that will affect all branches of medicine. Those who hold this belief claim that the demand for various practitioners will increase as the supply decreases. However, as we have seen in Chapter 3, the number of medical students admitted has been on the upswing in recent years. Even so, those who foresee a shortage of doctors point to trends that have fueled the demand for physicians: more people are living to a ripe old age with a corresponding increase in the demand for medical services as they become more vulnerable to disease and illness; elimination of such former killers as polio and diphtheria has increased the life span; and demand for health-care services is rising as more and more people are covered by such programs as HMOs, alternative health-care plans and, of course, the federal government.

All of these factors point to an increasing demand for doctors in all specialties. Certainly changes in medical technology will have a strong effect. For instance, the availability of such diagnostic tests as cardiac catheterization has heightened the demand for cardiologists with the skills to perform these services; availability of such tests as CT scans, MRIs, and nuclear scans has added to the demand for radiologists able to perform these tests.

Despite the uncertainty, it seems safe to predict that within ten to twenty years there will be tremendously expanded need for physicians with primary care credentials in pediatrics, internal medicine, geriatrics, preventive medicine, and adolescent psychiatry—while demand for practitioners in such fields as cardiology, gastroenterology, and anesthesia will taper down and even create surpluses. Even so, those who prefer the latter specialties can expect to find employment.

THE NEXT STEP: GAINING INFORMATION AND EXPERIENCE

Taking all of this into consideration—earnings, all the factors that can impact payment schedules, and anticipated demand of physicians—what should be your next step in choosing a specialty? The answer: to gather all of the information and experience you can in your specialty of interest. Here, right at the outset, one of the most important steps you can take is to choose a mentor or adviser. He or she can make a big difference in shaping your career by cluing you in to options that you might otherwise miss and helping you to get through the confusing and often gray areas of medicine.

Ask around, especially with those who are themselves going through the clinical circuit, who the top teachers are. Then try to select as your adviser one who is primarily a teacher, rather than someone involved largely in research, which can affect his or her availability as an adviser.

A truly top-notch adviser is one who is concerned with your future—who wants you to succeed at all costs. Such a person will make a great adviser.

Try to choose someone from a field similar to the one you are thinking of entering. A pediatrician or one specializing in geriatrics, for example, is not too far removed from an internist, but a radiologist or pathologist is worlds removed from an internist in most cases.

Now try to find opportunities to test your specialty preference. An excellent way to do this is to volunteer for clinical service when an experienced practitioner is on duty. Your adviser can help if he or she is in the clinical field in which you are interested; if not, he or she may be able to put you in touch with a person who has the authority to let you volunteer.

Here is an excellent way to check your initial reactions to a given specialty. Do the specialists in the field seem happy with what they are doing? Does the field offer the opportunity for professional growth, fulfillment, and income that you seek? What drawbacks, if any, can you detect? The sooner you become involved in your primary field of interest, the better your chances to really learn what the field is all about.

This is also a chance to test out your basic science studies to see how they apply in a clinical science setting. Talk to as many physicians in your specialty of preference as you can. Try to observe them in their offices, with patients, or in a clinical setting, hospital, or nursing home. Talking to the physicians involved and observing them at work under various conditions are excellent ways to learn about the field.

GETTING A RESIDENCY

Once you have decided on the specialty of particular appeal to you, you are ready to concentrate on the task of getting a residency. As mentioned previously there are approximately one thousand hospitals in the United States and Canada that offer some seven thousand residencies in all fields to qualified medical school graduates. And of all medical school graduates, who are now M.D.s, some 98 percent go on to do a residency in their chosen specialty, and in a few cases, several residencies. In this chapter we will list some of the factors that go into choosing a residency that is right for you, how to obtain information on residencies, what to look for in a residency, and so forth. But before we get into the nitty-gritty of choosing a residency, we'll discuss a few facts about the residency itself.

We bring this up because the residency is probably the most controversial aspect of getting a post–medical school education in your specialty. In most programs, residents were formerly on duty from eighty to one hundred and more hours per week and on call (available for duty) at least every third day. This has been the traditional setup on residencies in the United States and Canada ever since the Flexner Report stipulated curriculum and programs applying to residency programs in the United States and Canada.

While the long hours and low pay for residents have prevailed almost from the outset of medical education, in recent years several lawsuits have been initiated by residents and fellows (medical graduates studying for subspecialties of medicine). Several of these lawsuits, including one started by residents at the University of Alabama at Birmingham medical school in 2003, are still pending. In October of 2004, the U.S. Occupational Safety and Health Administration rejected a petition from Public Citizen, the Council of Interns and Residents, the American Medical Student Association, and several other groups urging federal regulation of resident work hours.

Besides the lawsuit begun by residents at the University of Alabama at Birmingham, several other suits have been started by the residents, including one begun in August 2003 that maintains that the "National Resident Matching Program has kept salaries artificially low . . . and crushes any competition that might force teaching hospitals to offer better conditions like shorter working hours." Even so, the fact remains that the National Resident Matching Program (also known as the Match) remains the primary means of matching teaching hospitals and graduates of medical schools looking for residencies.

But perhaps the most important edict of all in the area of residency hours was a recent ruling of the Accreditation Council for Graduate Medical Education (ACGME), which calls for a limit of eighty hours per week, among other changes. Residency programs that fail to comply with the standards mandated can be placed on probation or have their accreditation withdrawn. Among others the new standards call for:

- Residents are to receive one day out of seven free from all clinical duties averaged out over four weeks.
- On-duty periods cannot be scheduled for more than twenty-four consecutive hours, but can include up to six additional hours to transfer patients to new medical teams.
- Residents cannot be scheduled for call more than once every three nights, averaged over four weeks.

HOW TO GET THE RESIDENCY THAT SUITS YOU BEST

Once you have chosen the specialty in which you would like to practice, you should be concentrating on the task of getting a residency. The importance of this job cannot be overemphasized because you cannot be certified or licensed without completing a residency.

To accomplish this, there are a few things you should do while still in medical school. Here the question of grades, specifically honors grades, usually the equivalent of a straight A average, or 4.0 on a scale of 1 to 4, is the key factor.

While grades are important in all areas of medical school, they are especially so if you expect to obtain the residency most suited to your interests. If your school is one of the many on the pass/fail system, you will have to find other ways of showing your academic ability—such as special awards or letters of recommendation, for example.

Areas of special interest that are crucial are listed in order of importance, as follows:

1. **Third-year clerkships.** The experience you obtain during the clinical years is very similar in most medical schools, unlike your experience in the basic science years, where courses and teaching approaches can vary considerably.
2. **Senior specialty clerkships.** This clerkship is next in importance to your performance during the junior clerkships. It is especially important that you take a clerkship in a specialty of your choice in a major teaching hospital that is known and respected by residency directors.

3. **Basic science or preclinical years.** Especially important if you favor pathology because pathology is required in nearly all schools in the preclinical years.

One final comment about honors: while you don't have to be a genius to rate honors in any given course, it does take effort and plenty of it. Such things as coming in early for clinical rounds and staying late can get you extra credit from the house staff, as the residents in training are called.

You might also include extracurricular reading in the area of your clerkship or assignment and study diligently for any exams that may be required to complete your clerkship. By showing your willingness to go the extra mile, your efforts will pay off, all things being equal.

THE LICENSING EXAM AND OTHER FACTORS

Another way to ensure that you get the residency of your choice is to do well on the United States Medical Licensing Exam (USMLE), the three-step examination for licensure in the United States that replaces the Federation Licensing Examination (FLEX). Each part of this test measures your comprehension of the medical education curriculum. Step 1, for instance, given at the end of the basic science years, measures your understanding and ability to apply key concepts in biomedical sciences while step 2, given at the completion of the clinical years, evaluates your medical understanding and comprehension of clinical science in rendering patient care. Step 3, given after you finish medical school, assesses not only your comprehension of medical science, but your ability to apply that knowledge in a clinical setting.

These exams are used officially to determine qualification to practice medicine in nearly all states, and they are also used by many, if not most, of the residency programs in evaluating your credentials. An estimated 60 percent of all residency programs want to see how well you have done in step 1 of the USMLE, usually taken at the end of your sophomore year in medical school. And an estimated 40 percent of all residency programs want to see how well you do in step 2, taken either in April or September of your junior year. Note that currently the exam is limited to graduates of officially accredited medical schools in the United States or Canada; it excludes foreign medical students or graduates.

You cannot overestimate the importance of these exams because many residency program directors rely heavily on how well students do in these tests to screen applicants simply because it is probably the most objective proof of ability and attainment in medicine, much more reliable than dean's letters, and doubly important if your school is on the pass/fail system. Unless you can reach a minimum level of competency, as measured by the residency program involved (this varies from one specialty to another), you will most likely not be accepted by the program.

Today the USMLE has replaced the National Board of Medical Examiners (NBME) as an indicator of how well you have done in medical school, and it is expected to be as effective in screening applicants as was the NBME.

In addition to excelling in your clinical work and trying hard to earn honors in courses that can enhance your efforts to gain a residency, you should consider using your summer vacation to familiarize yourself with the world of clinical medicine. Besides serving as an escape from the regimentation of class work, such a move would provide the opportunity to practice medicine, although on a very limited scale. Ask your adviser or the student affairs office to help you locate such summer opportunities in clinical settings.

Note that research, though not absolutely necessary to obtain most residencies, can help in some areas where the competition is especially rough, such as ophthalmology, emergency medicine, or orthopedics. But if you are not that skilled in research, don't worry about it for now. Other opportunities will arise later, after you have landed a residency. You can then reevaluate your thinking about research.

A few more words about preparing for the residency before taking the next step: one important subject that is constantly being debated is the need for taking a senior clerkship in your specialty choice. Those who oppose such action say that it is senseless to duplicate the training you will receive during the residency itself. But if you are a top-grade student, such a clerkship could help to prove that you have what it takes to succeed in this specialty—not just the paper qualifications. If, on the other hand, your grades are not up to snuff to automatically place you in the running for a residency, then you will need to take a senior clerkship and earn top grades in it so you will even get a chance to be considered for a residency.

FINDING OUT ABOUT RESIDENCIES

At this point you should be starting to obtain information about residencies available in your choice of specialty. Such information should include what the residencies are like, how tough they are to get into, and options available for completing the program.

The two major sources of such information should be available through the student affairs office at your school. First is an annually updated computer program, the AMA Fellowship and Residency Electronic Interactive Database Access System (FREIDA for short), which provides information on such items as the characteristics of faculty and residents, call schedules, benefits, curriculum, shared off-schedule positions available, and much more.

Another valuable book is the *Directory of Graduate Education Programs*, often referred to as the Green Book, which is also updated annually by the AMA. Though not as detailed as the information contained in FREIDA, this source provides information not included in the database at present, including requirements for program accreditation, statistics on graduate medical information, specialty certification requirements, and so forth.

Another very valuable resource not included in either of the above directories is the *Medical Education* issue of the *Journal of the American Medical Association*, usually available in late summer or early fall. It provides a complete rundown on residency programs available, subspecialty and combined specialty residency programs, programs and residents on duty, and much more. All programs shown are accredited by the Accreditation Council for Graduate Medical Education. There were a total of 7,878 accredited programs at the end of 2004—3,964 relating to the core specialties and 3,914 for subspecialties.

In the fall of your senior year, you will receive the NRMP (National Residency Matching Program) directory, which lists programs participating in the Match, described later in this chapter, via the dean's office. This book explains how the Match works, code numbers and number of positions offered, and worksheets and forms needed to participate. The *NRMP Results* book gives the previous year's results and should be available in your school library and/or the student affairs office.

The Council of Teaching Hospitals Directory, published annually by the AAMC and available through that organization, offers much more detailed information about the residencies offered by members of the council than that found in the Green Book.

The American Hospital Association Guide to the Health Care Field, published by the AHA, offers information on the more than seven thousand member hospitals of the association. Though most are not primary or base teaching hospitals, a good part of your training could be received in many of these hospitals, and this could be a very helpful reference.

The Council of Teaching Hospitals conducts an annual survey of stipends, benefits, and funding for house staff, which can prove useful in evaluating residency programs. It is available from the AAMC.

Then too five specialties—family practice, preventive medicine, psychiatry, critical care medicine, and physical medicine and rehabilitation—publish detailed information on residency programs offered in each specialty. And the American Medical Student Association (see Appendix B) publishes the *Student Guide to the Appraisal and Selection of House Staff Training Programs*, which is packed with information on résumés, letters of recommendation, interviewing, and more.

For information about residencies in each specialty, write to the individual specialty society at the address shown in Appendix B.

WHAT TO LOOK FOR IN A RESIDENCY

The main thing to look for in considering residencies offered at a teaching hospital or clinic is the experience provided—both in the number and the type of patients and the setting. Find out the ratio of residents to patients seen. There may be too many residents to get any meaningful experience or too few residents, which means simply that you will not have enough time to evaluate patients and to discuss possible diagnoses and treatments. Setting is an important factor also. In a large teaching hospital there may be too few attending physicians and too many patients; the opposite may be true of many community hospitals.

- **On call schedules.** Although recent court rulings have tended to liberalize on call schedules, there are still many programs where night call every night is still common. Get the facts so that you can consider this very important issue.

- **Geographical location.** This could be an important decision if your spouse's work is confined to any given area. If you are single, the only restrictions on location are your own personal preferences.
- **Faculty.** Are the faculty interested primarily in teaching? Are there enough of them to do the job? Also, are there adequate opportunities in research to help you evaluate your interest in this area and to stay up-to-date on what is happening in the field?
- **Other considerations.** Another key factor involves opportunities to be exposed to a given area of a specialty that might be of interest, such as obstetrical anesthesiology as part of your anesthesiology residency. You will also want to find out about local job prospects after training, rules and benefits of health coverage for you and your family, if this applies, and insurance coverage.

You might also want to look into other benefits such as life and disability insurance, free parking, child care (if you have children), and opportunities to moonlight. Salaries do vary slightly for house staff by section of the country, and from private to public hospitals, which as a rule pay less. So be sure you check this out too.

HOW AND WHERE TO APPLY

The number of programs you should apply to will depend on your specialty. Generally, the more competitive the program, the more programs you should apply to. According to the AAMC, 48 percent of all medical students applied to six to fifteen programs in 2004, and 21.5 percent applied to sixteen to twenty-five programs. By contacting several programs, you can select the ones that best meet your needs; or if you go through the Match program, which most graduates do, you can select the programs of greatest appeal and hope that you get your preference.

In requesting information on the programs of interest, you will invariably receive a package containing information about the program and materials required, which can vary a lot from one program to another. You will also receive the required application. Most programs prefer that you fill out the application and send it with the materials requested—dean's letter, other reference letters, medical school and undergraduate transcripts, and other information. A few programs, however, use what is known as a Uniform Application Form.

As a rule, the earlier you get the information sent in, the better. Many programs have only so many openings for interviews, and if you wait too long (beyond August or September of your senior year) you may miss out on an interview.

Try to get at least one letter of recommendation from a faculty member of your chosen specialty. Other letters should come from faculty members who know you and can write enthusiastically about your abilities. Here again if a teacher seems at all hesitant about writing a letter, forget about it and contact someone else. If a faculty member has connections with a program of interest, this could be an extra bonus because such ties can be very useful.

Even if the program does not request it, be sure to enclose a copy of your résumé. It should be neat, concise, and accurate and should emphasize your strengths. It should in addition be well laid out and printed on good paper. Your adviser may be able to help in this important assignment by furnishing sample résumés or referring you to any of several fine references for use in preparing a résumé.

If you are a Canadian student, you may encounter some resistance in applying for residencies in the United States because of difficulties in comparing Canadian and United States applicants due to differences in the educational systems. You might be able to overcome this somewhat by including as much information as you can on your training, honors, and so forth. But even before you submit your application and support material, find out if the program will even consider Canadian applicants.

INTERVIEWS

Once applications have been submitted, you should be hearing soon from the programs you applied for. Here you should realize that the later in the season you schedule the interview, the better. There are two reasons for this: first, the screening process for prospective residents tends to be somewhat tougher in the beginning, but with the passage of time it tends to become somewhat more relaxed as the program directors get a more realistic handle on the current pool of applicants and their backgrounds. Second, interviewers tend to remember best those whom they have reviewed most recently when they decide who is to get the residencies.

As was true of interviewing for medical school, try to group your residency interviews by section of the country. It works out much better in terms of time and cost. Also, it's a good idea to have a few interviews under your belt before you try for the really big ones—those that you have ranked at the top of your list. This way you can polish your interviewing technique somewhat before going on an interview for one of your preferred residencies.

Now, having applied for residencies in about a dozen programs and received invitations for interviews from nearly half, what's next? There are several things you should take care of before going on an interview that can stack the deck in your favor.

First, research the school so that you have a pretty good idea of its clinical and academic facilities and faculty; then list the questions you want answered, including the type of students sought and the personal qualities desired—such as leadership, community involvement, and research or clinical ability.

Then review your application and support materials to make sure you can answer the questions that may arise concerning your background and record.

Schedule your interview at a time when you can attend morning rounds or a teaching conference. If possible, stay a day extra to talk to residents, especially those from your school. Quite often this is the best way to find out about strengths or weaknesses of the program that you could not obtain in any other way.

Bear in mind that the interview could lead to a paying job, so take it seriously. As was true when you interviewed for medical school, make sure that you dress conservatively in a suit. Men should wear a white or blue shirt and a neat tie. Avoid loud colors or flashing rings, watches, or jewelry that might distract from the serious business at hand. Sweaters and casual slacks may do when you are on call, but they are hardly appropriate for an interview. You are interviewing for a professional position and should dress the part.

As to the actual interview itself, here are a few pointers to keep in mind. First and most important, be on time. Your interviewer's time is valuable, as is your own; a late arrival does not make for a good impression and is seldom, if ever, excusable. Give yourself plenty of time, even if you have to sit around for a half hour or more—better to come early than to be late.

Make sure that you get the name or names of those doing the interviewing, with the proper spelling. The department secretary can give you this information just before the interview. Ordinarily, you would see just one interviewer, but you as well as several other applicants may be interviewed by a few key people in the program. Look them all in the eye when you enter and greet each by name and with a firm handshake. Wait until all are seated (it's only common courtesy) before you sit down.

While you may not be able to answer every question you have during the interview, here are a few of the more commonly asked questions that you may well want to consider:

- Is the faculty stable—what is the faculty turnover? This is a fairly sensitive area, but a very important one nevertheless. Be careful when asking about it and back off if necessary.
- How much contact will you have with the faculty—that is how often will you be in the clinics, wards, or operating rooms where you can have some contact with them?
- Where are the graduates practicing? What kind of jobs are they handling? How have they done on the specialty board exams? (This is an excellent tip-off on the value of the program.) Does the program help graduates to find jobs?
- How much autonomy do residents have in patient care? How many patients do residents ordinarily handle?
- What requirements are there, other than clinical, in such areas as research and special projects; writing case reports, reviews, and abstracts; and administration? Such activities can help or they may detract from your clinical training depending on your goals— patient treatment, research, diagnoses, and so forth, but it pays to get the facts ahead of time.

Here are some more questions you might want to consider: What changes, if any, in the curriculum are you considering? How many hospitals participate in the program? What do residents like most and least about the program? What is the patient mix—that is how many are private, how many on Medicare or Medicaid, how many are admitted for surgery or for medical conditions, accidents, and emergencies? And by all means, ask about benefits offered—life and health insurance for both you and your family, if pertinent; vacation time, sick days, parking privileges, and maternity leave.

It would also be a good idea to get an idea of the number of female residents, married residents, and social activities, if any. Also, it's smart to find out how often you are on call (very important), what happens if you should become sick, and precisely what is expected of the house staff.

From the program's perspective, here are a number of questions you may well be called on to answer:

- What are your goals?
- Why did you choose this specialty?
- What programs have you applied to?
- What are your strengths and weaknesses?
- What can you contribute to the program?
- Are you interested in clinical medicine or in teaching or research?

Or you may be asked certain questions about the kind of person you are such as the following:

- What are your hobbies and interests?
- What are your likes and dislikes?

Questions like these may seem far removed from medicine but are designed to help the interviewer get to know you better. And interviewers may want to see how you handle these, so be prepared for some seemingly far-removed questions.

HOW WELL YOU DO UNDER PRESSURE

While some of the following questions may seem tricky, they are designed to see how well you react under pressure. What trends do you see for medicine in the next decade? What problems do you see for your specialty in the near future? What happens if you don't match in your specialty (asked to see if you have the foresight to have contingencies if this should happen)? Tell me about yourself. (Answer by being honest and brief and not too detailed. If further information is wanted, let the interviewer follow up on this.)

Some questions may be personal, such as those regarding your family, which are illegal but nevertheless may be asked, especially if you are a woman. How should you handle such questions if they arise? You could, of course, refuse to answer the questions on the ground that they are illegal. While this may be true, it would not be tactful or helpful. A better choice would be to try to shame the questioner by responding something like, "Is this question really relevant?" And another choice would be to answer somewhat ambiguously by saying something like, "I have no plans to have a family while on my residency."

Studies show that most program directors choose applicants they believe will do well clinically, without presenting too many problems; those who are reliable; those who rank high on the national board exams and have high class rankings and clinical honors in medical school; and those who interview well. If you fit into any or all of these categories, you have it pretty much made in getting a residency.

IT'S A MATCH

We come now to one of the most controversial aspects of finding a residency—the Match, which critics contend locks medical graduates into residencies in which they have no say on pay, hours worked, and so forth. While this may be true to some extent, it is a fact that the match rate for U.S. medical school seniors seeking first-year residencies was 92.9 percent in 2004 and has remained between 92 and 94 percent for the past twenty years. It is further true that more than 80 percent of matched applicants obtained one of their top three choices for residencies through the Match, which works as follows: First you, the graduate, must rank the various programs of interest in order of preference. Likewise, the programs have ranked applicants in order of priority. It remains to be seen if a match can be arranged between each applicant and a residency program. To accomplish this, the overwhelming majority of applicants and programs take part in a computerized program known as the National Resident Matching Program, or the Match. The program then considers the top choices of both students and programs and proceeds to match them by order of preference. Initiated in 1952, it has taken many years to perfect—and despite its critics, the program does work as seen from the high percentage of students who are matched, as noted previously.

More than 80 percent of all matched applicants obtained one of their top three residency program choices. Matched U.S. medical school seniors attained a similar high success rate, as more than 85 percent were paired with one of their top three program choices. Of the 25,246 active applicants who participated in the Match in 2004, more than 20,000 matches were made to first- and second-year residency positions.

While the Match program is the overwhelming choice of most medical school graduates, it should be noted that despite this high rate of success, more than nine medical specialties run their own separate matching programs for filling residencies: ophthalmology, neurology, plastic surgery, preventive medicine, radiation oncology, otolaryngology, urology, neurosurgery, and nuclear medicine. Contact these specialty societies directly to obtain information on residencies that they offer (see Appendix B for their addresses).

Currently osteopathic medical school graduates have no matching programs to fill residency programs. Osteopathic students interested in postgraduate training in several specialties approved by the American Osteopathic Association (AOA; see Appendix B) participate in a registration program called the Intern Registration Program. Here students and programs do their own negotiating to see if they can work out agreements for specialty training during the student's senior year. In 2004 there were 223 AOA-approved programs that had 2,743 interns in training; there were in addition 555 residency training programs with 4,984 residency positions.

In nearly all first-year programs in family practice, general surgery, internal medicine, obstetrics-gynecology, pediatrics, and pathology, as well as first-year positions in psychiatry and emergency medicine, you can negotiate directly with the program about your specialty preference. (See appendix B for a list of specialty boards to contact.)

A few transitional programs offer first-year training in several specialties prior to your having to apply for a second year in a specific specialty. Then too a few programs in anesthesiology, neurology, nuclear medicine, ophthalmology, orthopedic surgery, otolaryngology, physical medicine, and neurological surgery offer a first year in internal medicine and general surgery prior to entering training in their specialties.

The NRMP also offers separate matching programs for residencies in dermatology and emergency medicine and, in addition, offers a number of fellowship programs providing training in various subspecialties. These are limited to those who have completed training in various core specialties involved. The Medical Specialties Matching Program (MSMP) offers fellowships in internal medicine subspecialties of cardiology, gastroenterology, and pulmonary diseases; colon and rectal surgery; foot and ankle surgery; general vascular surgery; hand surgery; pediatric ophthalmology; and thoracic surgery.

Medical graduates who participate in armed forces training programs will be involved in a separate match for residency programs offered by the military.

What it boils down to is this: if you have decided on a specialty, you need to find out if the specialty has its own match outside of the NRMP, if some programs are in the NRMP and some are not, or if all of the programs participate in the NRMP. You then must sign the NRMP participation form before the July deadline, at the end of your third year. It must be accompanied by a nonrefundable application fee ($25 in 2004). You can then rank ten hospitals on your rank order list; if you want to rank more, you must pay an additional fee for each program ranked.

Canadian medical graduates participate in their own matching program—the Canadian Intern Matching Service (CIMS)—or the NRMP. If you decide to match through the CIMS, your name is automatically removed from the list of candidates for the NRMP.

Graduates from schools approved by the American Osteopathic Association can also participate in the NRMP, but you should first check with the state because matches thus obtained do not automatically qualify osteopathic graduates for licensure in most states. In that way you can make certain that you have not gone through the Match in vain.

Results of the Match program are released in late March, on the same date for all Match participants, and are binding on both applicants and programs, just as if they had signed contracts for the residency.

While the overwhelming majority of students seeking residencies find their spots through the NRMP, it is estimated that more than a fifth of residents in training did not use the Match. These were graduates who for the most part found residencies through matching programs sponsored by an individual specialty not participating in the NRMP.

If you are among the five thousand or so medical graduates who participate in the Match and do not match, it may not be the worst thing that could happen. Your school may be able to help match you with programs that still have openings. A day or so prior to official notification of Match results, you will be notified if you failed to match. You are then free to seek out open residency slots, and for this purpose you will receive a booklet of spots that are unfilled. You then have a very brief period to review these spots, list your preferred choices, and to contact these programs by phone or e-mail. Since time is running out, you should be able to conclude negotiations right on the spot. You may have to fax or e-mail the program director a copy of your transcript, dean's letter, and other support materials, but it shouldn't be necessary to come in for an interview at this time of the game. In fact, you should be wary of any program that requires such an interview before offering you a contract.

CERTIFICATION AND LICENSURE

From the time you complete your residency and fellowship, training in various subspecialties that follows completion of residency training, it's only a short step to certification as a specialist and then to licensure.

To be certified you must have completed a residency of from two to five years in length, depending on the specialty, and an additional length of training for a subspecialty. You must then pass the board examination before you can be certified in that specific specialty.

For licensure for both D.O.s and M.D.s, you must first graduate from an accredited medical school, complete the licensing examination, and have participated in an accredited residency/internship training program.

At long last you will be ready to hang out your shingle as a licensed and board certified physician, either as a private practitioner or as a member of a group practice. In Chapter 7, we will discuss the options you have either as a solo practitioner or as a member of a group.

CHAPTER

6

A LOOK AT OSTEOPATHIC MEDICINE

Until now, we have confined our remarks to mainstream medicine, although they apply with equal accuracy to the other branch of medicine—osteopathic medicine—which is small, but nevertheless influential.

Active practitioners of osteopathic medicine, known as D.O.s (doctors of osteopathic medicine), now number about forty-nine thousand or around 7 percent of the physicians practicing in the United States and Canada. While fewer in number than allopathic (or mainstream medicine) doctors, D.O.s are very influential in states where they predominate—California, Illinois, Michigan, New Jersey, New York, Ohio, Pennsylvania, and Texas. Unlike their M.D. counterparts, osteopathic physicians tend to practice in primary care areas such as family practice, pediatrics, obstetrics-gynecology, and internal medicine. An estimated 10 percent of all D.O.s practice in communities of fewer than fifty thousand residents, as compared with about 1 percent of their allopathic counterparts. In many communities, D.O.s are the principal health-care providers. Nearly 40 percent specialize in twenty medical specialties, as compared with 65 percent of all M.D.s, who specialize in about twenty-four specialties and more than sixty-six subspecialties.

Even though their training and the training period involved—four years—are the same as that of M.D.s, osteopathic physicians are graduates of colleges of osteopathic medicine, of which there are twenty with two branches in the United States. There are none at this time in Canada, where the profession has not yet been formally organized. D.O.s are not chiropractors, bone specialists, or podiatrists, all of whom are more restricted in their powers of treatment and diagnosis.

Like their M.D. colleagues, osteopathic physicians are fully licensed to practice medicine in all its branches in all fifty states; prescribe drugs; admit patients to hospitals, both allopathic and osteopathic; perform surgery; deliver babies; and prescribe all of the commonly accepted forms of therapy including diet, physical and occupational therapy, and radiation.

WHERE D.O.S AND M.D.S DIFFER

Nevertheless there are some fundamental differences in outlook and approach to medicine between the two branches. D.O.s emphasize the interdependence of all body systems, including the musculoskeletal system. They also believe that imbalances in one body system can cause changes in function in others.

Osteopathic medicine places greater emphasis on holistic medicine, which is based on the interdependence of the body's organs and systems. What's more D.O.s, bring a unique hands-on approach to medicine and consider osteopathic spinal manipulation (OMT) a basic tool in the diagnosis and treatment of disease. Osteopathy also places greater importance on preventive medicine, proper nutrition, and staying fit.

D.O.s further emphasize the body's innate ability to stay healthy and its capacity to heal itself. As a result, osteopathic medicine strives to assist, support, and sometimes to spark the body's natural tendencies to maintain its own health.

WHAT IT TAKES TO BECOME A D.O.

Like mainstream medicine, osteopathic medicine requires that candidates for medical school have three years of undergraduate college or a bachelor's degree. The required courses are very much like those of allopathic medicine—usually one year each of English, biological sciences, physics, general chemistry, and organic chemistry. A few schools also require courses in genetics, math, and psychology.

Also, while most D.O.s major in science, chemistry, or biology, they can major in other areas, including the humanities, as long as they get good grades and can show good credentials in science and in the MCAT. Finally, as is true of their allopathic counterparts, osteopathic colleges require a personal interview to evaluate your social and interpersonal skills and to see if you have the necessary motivation to do well in the very long and grueling curriculum leading to a medical degree.

But the resemblance does not end there because the academic programs of osteopathic medicine and allopathic medicine are about the same. The first two years in osteopathic medical schools—like their allopathic counterparts—stress anatomy, physiology, biochemistry, microbiology, pathology, and pharmacology.

And as in the training of M.D.s, osteopathic medicine stresses clinical subjects—involving the treatment of patients—in the last two years of medical school. Included are such subjects as medicine, pediatrics, obstetrics and gynecology, radiation, and surgery, and revolving clerkships through various subject areas in the student's third year, the same as allopathic medicine.

Mixed in throughout the four-year medical program are courses stressing osteopathic principles and techniques. Following graduation, an American Osteopathic Association (AOA)–approved internship of twelve months is required. From there, as is true of M.D.s, students go on to a residency in various specialties requiring from two to five years of additional training.

While the number of AOA-approved residencies has risen in recent years, there are still not enough to handle the need, so many osteopathic medical graduates take M.D.-approved residencies for their specialty training.

However, before you can practice, you, like your M.D. colleagues, must obtain a license from the state licensing board. Boards vary in their makeup. Some are composed entirely of D.O.s and others of M.D.s, while others are composed of a combination of the two.

Requirements for licensure for both D.O.s and M.D.s are about the same in all states and grant osteopathic physicians full practice rights as physicians.

Once in practice, D.O.s can be admitted to any of two hundred osteopathic hospitals located in twenty-eight states, and increasingly D.O.s are being admitted to M.D.-controlled hospitals as well.

Since the two branches are so similar, the federal government and state governments, as well as public and private health agencies, consider osteopathic medicine as a separate but equal branch of medicine. Since D.O.s have all the rights and professional standing of their M.D. associates, many have been admitted to M.D.-controlled state, local, and national medical societies.

D.O.s also serve as commissioned officers in all branches of the armed forces. They may serve as medical officers in the civil service, U.S. Public Health Service, and the Department of Veterans Affairs.

WHY TWO BRANCHES OF MEDICINE?

With so many points of similarity, you may well ask why osteopathic medicine maintains its own superstructure—professional organizations, including the American Osteopathic Association; separate but equal medical schools; and separate but equal osteopathic hospitals, specialty societies, and certifying boards. Wouldn't it make sense for the two branches of medicine to merge into one united medical body?

To which osteopathy answers: By combining osteopathic principles with traditional diagnostic and treatment procedures, D.O.s offer a unique system of health care aimed at preventing and curing disease. And by treating the whole person, not just the disease, the D.O. seeks to improve the quality of care for all patients. The profession also points to the great strides osteopathic medicine has made in recent years. The number of D.O.s has risen from thirty thousand in 1991 to forty-nine thousand today. With this increase in numbers has come increased public acceptance of osteopathic physicians as well. Although osteopathic medicine works with allopathic medicine in seeking to upgrade the standards of health care in the United States, it does have its own approach and prefers to stay a separate but equal branch of medicine.

THE BEGINNING OF OSTEOPATHY

How did osteopathy reach its present prominent status in medicine? The origins of the profession go back to 1874, to the frontier Missouri town of Kirksville. There, a courageous and determined M.D. named Andrew Still was becoming increasingly disenchanted with nineteenth-century mainstream medicine. He was dissatisfied with the very rudimentary drugs and surgery available to treat disease, especially after losing three of his own children. At the time, in the 1870s, anesthesia, sterile surgery, and antiseptics were unknown on the frontier, and x-rays and antibiotics were undreamt of.

To combat the inadequacies of the medicine of the time, Dr. Still founded his own unique brand of medicine, built around the philosophy of Hippocrates, who is often called the father of medicine. The central focus of Dr. Still's new system was the unity of the body. As the distinguishing feature in maintaining the body's health, he identified the musculoskeletal system, which was the key to his concept of medicine—a concept that is receiving widespread acceptance in mainstream medicine today.

To make his new concept of medicine more acceptable and to make for a more effective medical treatment, Dr. Still stressed palpation and human touch. He offered spinal manipulation as a less intrusive form of diagnosis and treatment, a concept that has been increasingly embraced by the American public. Today osteopathic medicine offers the full gamut of medical diagnosis and treatment and D.O.s are physicians in the full sense of the term.

HOW OSTEOPATHY WORKS

To see how osteopathy works, let's examine a few typical medical cases and how they would be treated by an osteopathic physician.

For example, the surgical removal of a diseased gallbladder is accepted practice by all physicians, but D.O.s believe that medicine should do more than merely repair, remove, or relieve the diseased organ. To the D.O., the gallbladder does not function independently; its nerve and blood supplies are also involved in maintaining the chemical balance of body fluids. So besides treating the critical phase of the disease, the D.O. is concerned with returning the patient to full health by treating the internal and external conditions that caused the disease in the first place.

This is not to imply that the M.D. is not concerned with the underlying causes of disease, but it is simply that in osteopathic medicine, students are conditioned to be on the lookout for the underlying causes of disease.

The D.O. has several corrective methods that are unique. They may take the form of palpation as a diagnostic procedure to detect soft tissue changes or structural defects in the body; at other times they may be seen as a form of corrective manipulation to relieve dysfunction of limited motion of the joints. Since musculoskeletal dysfunctions can mimic other disease symptoms, osteopathic manipulation can contribute greatly to the diagnosis and treatment of structural problems.

For example, it is known that diseases of specific organs can produce pain in remote areas of the body. Stomach ulcers, for instance, can produce areas of spinal pain just below the shoulders in the back. The spread of pain to the loin from a diseased kidney is yet another example, as is the radiation of pain to the left shoulder as a symptom of heart disease. D.O.s are trained to recognize that symptoms can be mimicked in these other areas to which the pain has been transferred.

Or consider that it is a known fact that disorders of the spinal column can cause recurrent headaches. If you properly apply manipulative therapy, especially to the neck and head, quite often you can relieve the headache symptoms. This is an example of how osteopathic medicine, through the holistic principle, strives to maintain peak health in all body organs.

THE FUTURE OF OSTEOPATHIC MEDICINE

As to the future of the profession, while nothing is for sure, the signs for continued growth and prosperity for the individual D.O. are brighter, if anything, than for medicine as a whole. Longer life spans and correspondingly greater need for health care, as well as the emphasis on insurance and federally funded programs to pay for the cost of medical care, all point to a greater need for physicians. And as is true of the M.D., the greatest need is for primary care physicians—general practitioners, internists, pediatricians, and obstetrician-gynecologists. Since an estimated three-fourths of all osteopathic physicians fall into the category of primary health care, the outlook for continued demand for D.O. services is indeed bright.

In addition, the fact that many D.O.s prefer to practice in smaller communities, where the demand for medical care is greatest, is yet another reason to expect continued growth in the profession during the next decade.

CHAPTER

7

LAUNCHING A PRACTICE AND GETTING AHEAD

With your license and medical school diploma in hand and a board certification in your specialty, you're ready to start a practice, right? Wrong. There is still another very important decision you've got to make: do you strike out on your own or take a salaried position? If you decide on a salaried position, is it temporary or with an HMO, group practice, or other organization? You have several options, and that's what we address in this chapter.

TAKING A PAID POSITION

Before we delve deeper into the paid position, let's review the pros and cons of taking a paid position or striking out on your own in a solo practice. Surveys of the AMA show that an estimated two-thirds of all new physicians choose to go the salary route—they choose to work for someone else. And there are many good reasons for this. First, it takes a certain amount of courage to go out on your own. It may take many long months until your practice takes hold. Chances are that you are already deeply in debt in your medical school training—about $115,000 on the average, while postmedical (residency) school debt now approaches more than $100,000. That's a heavy load, and for that reason alone, many graduates choose the safe route and take a job as a part of a group or working for an HMO, a surgicenter, hospital emergency room, staff position, or some other paying position. Then, too, the would-be solo practitioner—already deeply in debt—faces further debt in trying to raise the capital it takes to purchase equipment and furniture, sign a lease, order supplies, and pay for all of the other expenses he or she will face in organizing a new practice. In other words, it may take a substantial investment of many thousands of dollars just to get started in a solo practice, disregarding rent, insurance, and taxes that you would have to face in keeping the practice going. Still, as will be seen later in this chapter, many licensed physicians are entering solo practice, and there are many good reasons for this.

THE DOWNSIDE IN STARTING A SOLO PRACTICE

There are many other factors that might cause you to think twice about starting your own practice. For one, a new practice is a gamble and can be strongly affected by such outside forces as recession, inflation, unemployment, governmental restrictions, and the economy in general. Then too personal factors such as your health, energy, and skill in finding and keeping new patients, community relations, and solving family problems can also strongly influence the success of a practice.

Over and above these negatives are many other problems you will face in starting a new practice: longer hours than colleagues who are salaried, less time for vacations, difficulty in arranging coverage when you are on vacation or ill, and the need to meet overhead expenses—including insurance, telephone, electricity, secretarial wages, and rent—which must be paid whether or not you are busy.

Weighed against all of these disadvantages, the salaried position offers relief from all of this frustration and worry. Salaried physicians can hold positions in government agencies (federal, state, or local), private industry and commercial companies, insurance companies, the military (army, navy, air force, marines), and many other agencies. But perhaps the greatest number of openings for physicians, accounting for roughly 20 percent, is found in private or public hospitals where physicians are needed to staff the emergency room or act as consultant or staff person in such departments as occupational or pulmonary medicine. In addition, certain specialists such as pathologists, radiologists, and neonatologists (see Chapter 10) are almost always hospital based.

SALARIED VERSUS SOLO PRACTICE

The benefits of salaried employment are obvious: good security, attractive benefit packages, paid vacations and holidays, sick days, health coverage (medical as well as dental—not only for the doctor but for the entire family), the latest in medical equipment at hand, and a good salary, although chances are you could do better in solo practice.

Furthermore, as a salaried doctor you avoid all of the headaches and realize many benefits that you might not have otherwise. Health-care coverage, for example, is something that you as a solo practitioner would have to pay for and obtain on your own, either by joining a group, an HMO, or some other kind of insurance provider, the same as anyone else.

But you pay a price in taking a salaried job that you should strongly consider. For one, you give up a good part of your autonomy and professional independence. You are now subject to the whims, needs, and desires of your superiors. You are just a cog in the operation of the team and have limited, if any, say in the way the team operates.

And besides the loss of income, which is something you must consider, there is always the possibility of personality conflicts with higher-ups, associates, and patients to whom you can be assigned, all of which can be frustrating. But it should be noted that even if you practice solo, you could still face some of these frustrations, especially those involving patient hang-ups and problems.

On the other hand, as a paid employee, you work shorter hours than your self-employed counterpart and have a much better grip on your time off—vacations, holidays, and days off.

While taking a salaried position may be the preferred route of many starting physicians, the fact is that the situation can change radically in just a few years. According to the AMA, the number of salaried physicians drops sharply from 66.7 percent during the first two years of practice to 32.4 percent for those with six to eight years of practice and to only 27.5 percent for those with nine to eleven years of practice. But these are overall figures. The number of salaried physicians varies a lot by specialty, ranging from 100 percent of pathologists with two or fewer years of practice and 83 percent of radiologists with similar experience to 42.5 percent for psychiatrists and 51 percent for general surgeons.

Women are much more likely to opt for salaried positions than men. Although the percentage of women choosing salaried employment was only slightly higher in the first two years of practice, the decline was not nearly as sharp as it was for men. In the most experienced category, those with nineteen or more years of practice, women were much more likely to be salaried than men (35 percent as compared with 27 percent).

STARTING A SOLO PRACTICE

Solo practitioners, although not the force they once were in the profession, account for better than half of physicians currently practicing. What exactly is a solo practitioner? Donald M. Donahugh, in his book *Practice Management for Physicians*, puts it this way: "A solo practitioner is one who has a direct relationship with each patient. He provides professional services to the patient, is personally responsible for that care, and receives a fee in exchange for his services."

What is so appealing about having your own practice? As we have seen, there are several factors at work here, including greater autonomy and independence. Beyond that, there is the opportunity to establish a long-lasting and highly satisfying relationship with your patients, which is true of a salaried physician as well but probably not to the extent of the solo doctor, since as a salaried physician you have less control of what patients you see and when. There is also the possibility of losing a patient, but for most practitioners the former is much more likely than the latter.

As a solo physician, you are much more independent than your salaried colleagues. You choose your location, the office layout and design, color scheme, size, fees to charge, personnel, and everything else having to do with the practice. For better or worse, you are in charge. If things go right, great; but if not, you have no one to blame but yourself—or perhaps the economy. Ordinarily, after several lean years during which you are building your practice, you will peak to a salary comparable to what other M.D.s with similar experience and backgrounds command.

Long hours and difficulties in arranging coverage if you are ill or on a vacation are only part of what you'll need to worry about as a solo practitioner. You also need to consider the relative isolation that you'll experience, especially if your practice is located in a small or remote community. In such cases, you will need to go out of your way to find others to consult with about the best treatment or diagnosis for your patients. Most likely, you will have no business manager to handle the numerous forms that are required by government at all levels, as well as those of private pay insurance carriers and patients. It's a never-ending and often seemingly losing battle to keep up with all of the paperwork.

Today many old-time practitioners long for a return to the days when a physician had more command of his or her practice. Today the M.D. or D.O. is backstopped by federal and state governments in such programs as Medicare and Medicaid, by third-party payers (insurance companies), and by utilization review agencies that monitor whether or not a hospital admission is warranted or certain tests and procedures are necessary based on the diagnosis. But the nature of solo practice, in which the physician is his or her own boss, would indicate that the solo practice still has a lot going for it.

WORKING IN A GROUP PRACTICE

Let's face it, today group practice is the way physicians prefer practicing, and these groups are growing like wildfire. They are, to a great extent, replacing solo practitioners. Between 1965 and 1991, the number of physician groups almost quadrupled, from 4,289 to 13,000. And between 1991 and 1996 the number of groups had grown to 19,000, representing a 46 percent increase in just five years.

There are good reasons for this explosive growth in the number of groups. In a nutshell, they include sharing fixed costs (rent, insurance, taxes, and accounting costs), pooled revenues, better internal handling of patients (referrals to specialists and other doctors in the group best equipped to handle a given patient's needs), and better penetration of the local market (primarily recruitment of patients).

At the same time the number of solo practitioners has dropped from about 80 percent of the total number of active physicians in 1987 to about 50 percent today. This will give you some idea of which way the wind is blowing in medical practice.

Let's start by defining just what is meant by the term *group practice*. According to the AMA it is "the application of medical service by physicians formally organized to provide medical care, consultation, diagnosis, or treatment through the joint use of equipment and personnel with income from the medical practice distributed in accordance with methods previously agreed on by members of the group."

Although this generally describes a group practice, the exact nature of the group, how members are admitted, how revenues are distributed, and how expenses and other considerations are handled vary from group to group. A group may be an association of solo practitioners, a corporation, or a partnership. More than two-thirds of all group practices are incorporated, while most solo practices are not. The primary advantage of incorporation is that all assets and expenses of the group are part of the corporation. If a member of the group is sued for malpractice, the corporation as a whole cannot be sued, and its assets cannot be touched if he or she should lose.

By far the major trend in group practices today is integration into larger organizations, such as outright purchase of practices by hospitals, universities, staff model HMOs, and (most often) by other physicians. This also includes what is known as vertical integration through strategic alliances between a hospital and its medical staff.

THE POPULARITY OF GROUP PRACTICE

Why the big movement to group practices today? There are several reasons. Because group practice often represents a pooling of revenues and expenses of all members of the group, outlays for equipment, technical services, and facilities can be taken from revenues that are often far superior to what is available to the solo doctor. Utilization is better as well; because certain staff members of the group may have more patients than they can handle, it is possible to assign newer patients to other group members, particularly the newest physicians to join, who may not be so busy.

Coverage for vacations, weekends, and illness is more easily arranged because vacations and other time off are assigned in turn on a regularly scheduled basis to all members. Because coverage is assured, individual members can better plan their vacations and days off.

Then too members of the group as a rule work fewer hours per week than do solo doctors—about fifty-five hours compared to the fifty-eight-plus hours worked by solo practitioners. The hours are also more regular. In larger groups (five or more members), income is only slightly lower, if at all, than it is for self-employed physicians.

Still other advantages include the greater availability of office personnel to take care of the increasing number of ancillary services such as drawing blood and taking blood pressure. The group can more readily afford to hire a business manager experienced in personnel, office operations, and book-keeping to fill out the myriad forms required and to supervise all business phases of the practice—a luxury few solo physicians can enjoy.

In response, solo practitioners point to their greater independence in terms of not being bound by group restrictions that may not be to their liking. Also the group practitioner is subject to disagreements with other members of the practice, which can be annoying and frustrating. In the case of the solo practitioner, the practice rises or falls primarily on the ability of that physician.

As a member of a group, you are not only more restricted in your practice options, but also in possible income, because you are limited in the number of patients seen, hours when you can see them, and so forth.

These are the two primary options to consider in starting a medical practice; however, there are several others that should also be considered.

OTHER PRACTICE OPTIONS

The first option, a variation of solo practice, involves becoming associated with an older and more experienced physician who is seeking to cut down his or her practice and hours worked and eventually, perhaps, to sell the practice.

Such an association can be attractive to you as the physician seeking to become established and to the older physician as well. For the younger physician, it's a good way to become established in the community. As the senior physician introduces you to community residents, you immediately start to form relationships with many. And you have the opportunity to learn firsthand the business aspects of running a practice without being fully responsible for any mistakes you might make. The senior associate benefits by being able to cut down a little on the workload and hours, and at the same time enjoy lower costs.

In such an arrangement, it should be spelled out that this is a relationship of convenience and that senior and junior physicians have solo practices and are merely sharing expenses. Such associations almost always lead to a more formal arrangement if the participants are not compatible. Although the arrangement may not be bound by a formal contract, it is best that specifics of the association be spelled out by a written document or memorandum of understanding signed by both associates.

Quite often such an arrangement can work into a partnership between the two principals. In this case a legally binding document spelling out specifics of the arrangement—including the lease, equipment, personnel salaries, and who pays what for utilities and telephone—should be signed.

In many cases, the young physician may be able to purchase the practice through such an association. The advantage is that such an acquired practice offers a good location—one that is completely equipped. Often, the selling physician will act as consultant both as to the handling of the patients and the business side of the practice. Here it is essential that the doctor selling the practice know how to evaluate its worth correctly. This involves reviewing gross earnings, assets, lease, improvements, and goodwill, all of which are discussed in Dr. Donahugh's book, which is an excellent resource for help in evaluating an established practice.

WORKING FOR AN HMO

HMOs (health maintenance organizations) have become such a prominent part of medicine that they are an option you should consider in starting a practice. In most HMOs you would work for the HMO as a doctor, but in the IPA (independent practitioner association) arrangement, you are part of an associated group of physicians who provide medical services for the HMO. In an HMO, you have the option of signing on as a salaried physician or merely participating in the managed care program as an independent practitioner or as a member of a group. HMOs, or managed care programs (see Chapter 2), are sweeping the country and there are estimates that HMO membership will surpass one hundred million members by 2010. As many as 77 percent of all practicing physicians participate in some type of managed care program.

Basically there are three kinds of HMOs. The first is patterned after the pioneer programs, the Kaiser Permanente Plan and the Health Insurance Plan of Greater New York. Under this arrangement, the doctors involved are partners of the group and the success or failure is reflected directly in their success or failure.

The second category is the staff arrangement, where the doctors involved are salaried employees and do not participate in distribution of any profits, nor are they personally liable if the HMO fails to show a profit in any given year.

Under the third arrangement, the IPA, participants are loosely affiliated with the HMO and work on a part-time basis. For most participants in such an arrangement, the HMO supplies roughly 10 percent of their patients. Because the majority of the practice does not depend on the HMO, the doctors involved do not rely on the success of the plan. It is primarily a supplement to their basic practice.

Whatever type of arrangement you elect to follow in starting your practice—salaried group partnership, junior associate with a senior physician, and so forth—the details of the arrangement should be clearly spelled out in a letter of agreement or contract to avoid misunderstandings.

HOURS AND INCOME

Other considerations enter into your decision how to start out in practice. Hours vary with the practice. A recent survey by the Bureau of Labor Statistics showed that salaried physicians averaged fifty-two hours per week, as compared with fifty-eight hours per week for solo practitioners.

The impact of the type of specialty on the workweek is seen by the fact that according to the survey, in 2004, family physicians worked sixty-three hours a week. Another survey on the doctors' workweek by the Bureau of Labor Statistics showed that 32 percent worked fifty-five to ninety-nine hours per week, 24 percent worked forty-five to fifty-four hours per week, and 32 percent worked thirty-five to forty-four hours per week

Likewise salaries for doctors varied considerably by specialty. A recent physicians salary survey showed that in 2003 primary care physicians earned lower salaries than surgeons. Specifically, the survey showed that general or family practitioners averaged $152,478 per year; internists $159,978 a year; pediatricians $158,000 a year; and obstetrician-gynecologists 237,000 a year as compared with orthopedic surgeons, who averaged $397,000, which was exceeded only by radiologists, who averaged $403,000 per year.

Although such trends as the Resource-Based Relative Value Scale (RBRVS) have closed the gap somewhat between primary care physicians and specialists, there is no doubt that the gap will continue to exist.

GETTING STARTED

Where to start your practice is still another consideration. There is little doubt that where doctors do their residency will greatly affect where they practice. During residency, many residents receive offers from the attending staff who are looking for junior partners. Here the advantage is that the two physicians in joint practice know each other and their capabilities and are well equipped to decide if their years of working together would likely lead to success in a joint practice, either in an association of solo practitioners or in a partnership.

Besides this possibility, the local, state, national, and specialty society journals all run ads for physicians wanted and carry lists of new graduates seeking positions. If you are following up on an ad for a physician, you should by all means check out the opening by traveling to the area where the opening is located and discussing the position in person with the physician or physicians involved before making a commitment.

Physicians in a partnership work closely together, and though work habits, temperaments, and personalities may differ a lot, they may not show up until some time has elapsed. Or two physicians in a partnership may be quite different in how they treat patients, and the one seeing considerably more patients per session may be shortchanged if he or she is sharing equally in the partnership.

In addition to professional journals and medical societies, there are medical employment agencies that can help you to find a position.

Finally, if you are thinking of starting your own practice, you might well consider taking a part-time medical position to help tide you over until your practice requires your full attention and energy. For example, you might be able to find part-time employment in clinics that pay so much per session or in hospital outpatient departments or emergency rooms where you may be able to work evenings or on weekends while establishing your own practice during other hours.

A GLIMPSE OF THE FUTURE

There is so much happening in the field of medicine in the way of new treatments, diagnoses, and medications that it is almost impossible to predict what will happen in the future. Nevertheless, in this chapter we attempt to do just that: forecast what's in store for medicine in the immediate future.

The question of manpower is particularly tricky. Many experts have testified that the field is overcrowded, and at first glance it may seem so. According to M. Roy Schwartz, a former AMA group vice president of medical education and sciences, by 2010 the United States will have 163,000 more doctors than it needs. And the Council on Graduate Medical Education, an agency established by Congress, foresaw a surplus of 115,000 physicians by 2000.

A QUESTION OF MALDISTRIBUTION OR OVERSUPPLY

But to many, it's not so much a matter of oversupply but of maldistribution. For example, Massachusetts, Maryland, Pennsylvania, New York, and Connecticut all have more than three hundred M.D.s per hundred thousand population, while Idaho, South Dakota, and Wyoming had less than half as many doctors per hundred thousand population.

Possibly more of a factor is the oversupply of specialists including neurologists, cardiologists, gastroenterologists, and urologists. However, there is little doubt that primary care physicians—general practitioners, family practice doctors, pediatricians, and obstetrician-gynecologists—will be in great demand. Until recently the *doing*, or specialist oriented, areas of medicine commanded the larger salaries and the greater demand. But today the teaching hospitals are being rewarded by Medicare for reducing the number of residencies available for training medical specialists.

Further proof of maldistribution of doctors is seen in the rapidly shrinking numbers of physicians practicing in rural areas and in smaller communities—those of fewer than fifty thousand residents. In rural Illinois there are only four M.D.s for every thirty-five hundred residents, and the situation is even worse in primary care, where there is only one M.D. for the same. And what is true of Illinois is true to a great extent of many other states.

The shortage of doctors in rural areas is one reason why the osteopathic profession has begun to attract the number of students it has—since an estimated 20 percent will start their practices in communities of fewer than fifty thousand residents.

SALARIED JOBS ARE ON THE RISE

Just what this portends for the profession is not clear at present, but there is little doubt that salaried jobs for physicians, although already booming, will accelerate for reasons outlined in Chapter 7 relating to the cost of starting a solo practice.

Recent decades have witnessed the growth of group practices, with more and more doctors opting for salaried positions. It is believed that due to the efficiencies of group practices and managed care, such as HMOs, fewer physicians will be able to care for more patients, thus somewhat limiting the need for more physicians.

But this can be deceiving. Take cardiology, one of the most crowded specialties according to the Graduate Medical Education National Advisory Committee. Will the increased use of diagnostic tests such as cardiac catheterization, stress tests, and angiograms create a greater demand for cardiologists trained in these new techniques? And how will these new procedures affect cardiovascular surgeons in such procedures as bypass surgery or implanting of cardiac devices?

How will such relatively recent developments as the Resource-Based Relative Value Scale affect physicians? This new system, required by all third-party payers, reimburses physicians on a new scale taking into account time invested in a patient, cost of training the doctor, cost of the practice, and so forth.

In programs such as Medicare and Medicaid, both insurance companies and the government have tended to pay a premium for the so-called *doing* procedures, as seen in many areas of surgery, while the cognitive skills of primary care physicians have often been disregarded.

Will the emphasis on RBRVS reduce reimbursement inequities and make primary care more attractive for students? This remains a question. What about the physician Diagnosis Related Groups (DRGs)? This system, if launched, could further lower the income of many specialists. An extension of the current DRG plan, which is the basis for hospital reimbursement under Medicare, this system would group various diseases and diagnoses together and the physician would be paid a fixed amount regardless of the actual time invested in the patient or any unforeseen complications that could arise. This form of reimbursement, known as prospective payment, is now in effect in hospitals and is believed to be on the horizon for physicians.

MALPRACTICE: A GROWING TREND

Another factor that almost certainly will grow out of control in years to come is medical liability of malpractice. This is a real headache to many physicians—especially those in obstetrics-gynecology, dermatology, and pediatrics. In 2001, malpractice was a term of little importance to most physicians, but by the end of 2004 it had grown to proportions that threatened to swallow many practitioners whole, to hear them tell it, at least those in high-risk professions.

In Florida, voters recently approved the "three strikes" amendment to the state constitution that automatically revokes the license of any doctor with three malpractice judgments.

The AMA reports thirty-four states raised liability insurance rates 25 percent or more in 2004, nearly double the increase of the eighteen states that made similar hikes in liability in 2001.

Physicians in at least two states—Pennsylvania and West Virginia—have begun to factor the cost of liability insurance premiums into their charges.

The AMA cites many other examples of the negative effects soaring malpractice insurance rates have had on the profession. Physicians have moved from Texas, Pennsylvania, and Florida to low-rate states such as Oklahoma to avoid surging malpractice premiums. The past president of the Oklahoma State Medical Association now says, "We are seeing our physicians retiring early and stopping some high-risk procedures."

WOMEN: A GROWING FORCE IN MEDICINE

Another trend that is expected to accelerate involves the number of women accepted as medical students as well as those opening their own medical practices. Last year, 43 percent of all medical school graduates were women, and the numbers are expected to increase every year in the immediate future.

Today there are more than 225,000 female doctors in the United States. Deducting 28,000 who are categorized as inactive or unclassified, women still comprise about 26 percent of all physicians, up from 23 percent in 2000, which in turn was up from only about 12 percent of the total doctor population in 1980.

More than half of all female doctors practice in four primary care specialties—internal medicine, pediatrics, family practice, and obstetrics. In fact, today there are 16,257 women obstetrician-gynecologists, and women seem to be taking over this specialty.

Last year nearly 65 percent of ob-gyn residents were women, compared with only 16 percent in 1976. As one female neurologist at Northwestern Memorial Hospital put it, "Women do well in that kind of nurturing, supportive role." Surveys also have shown that compared with men, female doctors spend more time listening to patients, talk less, give patients more time to ask questions, and so forth. Interestingly, studies have shown that female doctors are also less likely to be sued for malpractice than male doctors.

One other factor that will take an ever more prominent role in medicine is alternative or integrative medicine. This is the area of medicine that includes such once-frowned-on practices as biofeedback, herbal medicine, chiropractic, naturopathy, acupuncture, and yoga, among others. Almost all of these fields of practice have, at one time or other, been fiercely denounced by mainstream medicine as quackery and frauds. Today integrative medicine is medicine's new flash word.

While at least a third of U.S. adults use complementary or alternative medicine, few doctors have integrated it into their practice. But in time medical professionals will resort to mainstream treatment in cancer, heart problems, and so forth, but rely more heavily on alternative medicine for patients with chronic problems such as irritable bowel, sinusitis, migraines, and high blood pressure. In general, medical graduates fresh out of medical school are more receptive to alternative forms of treatment than their older peers.

HEALTH-CARE COSTS ARE BOOMING

Another factor that is having an ever-increasing impact on the practice of medicine is rapidly expanding medical costs. Health-care spending in the United States was $1.4 trillion in 2004, as compared with $884 billion in 1993. Health care is by far the fastest growing component of the GNP, far outstripping food, shelter, and transportation.

It is a fact that the United States spends more on health care than other industrialized nations—13.9 of GNP compared to 9.5 percent in France, 9.7 percent in Canada, and 8.7 percent in Sweden. By 2006, economists figure the average family health insurance premium will exceed $14,000 per year and will have leapt by more than $5,000 in just three years.

What has triggered this explosion in health-care costs and usage? The reasons are many and complex. For one, there has been a tremendous acceleration in population growth. Thanks to medical science, people are living longer and are better able to withstand the ravages of diseases such as polio, pneumonia, diabetes, and hardening of the arteries, which only a few years ago most likely would have resulted in death or disability. Accompanying this rise in longevity has been an almost equal demand for medical care: the longer you live, the more vulnerable you become to potentially fatal and crippling diseases.

But beyond medical technology, it's a fact the great majority of Americans are covered by insurance—both private and public. Just a few decades ago, the overwhelming majority of Americans—estimated at 90 percent—paid for medical and health-care services out of their own pockets. Today the federal government (through Medicare, Medicaid, and other federally sponsored programs) and private insurance programs, including HMOs, foot more than 50 percent of the health-care bill, thus making health care available to millions. A few decades ago, many of us would have hesitated to see a doctor or even go to a hospital; today we think of both hospital and medical care as a right rather than something we have to pay for.

What it amounts to is that the government, as the largest health-care payer accounting for nearly 43 percent of the health-care dollar, has in recent years taken steps to stop the rise of health-care costs. Already we have seen the first step in that direction with the institution of the DRG system as the basis for payment of hospital bills under Medicare and the strong possibility of extending this to physicians' fees. Along with this new payment system has come the establishment of peer review groups to monitor hospital admissions, length of stay, and other activities. This is true not only of Medicare patients, but also to those covered by Medicaid (the state-operated health-care program for poor, or indigent, patients).

CYBERSPACE: THE HERE AND NOW OF MEDICINE

Accompanying this expansion of coverage has been a proportionate upsurge in our awareness of health-care services, including medical treatment, through the sharp increase in health-care publicity being given by the media. It is estimated that more Americans learn about new discoveries in medical care and treatment through the media than through their own doctors. Today it's almost certain that you can see or hear reporters that specialize in medicine and health care on the TV or radio and read their stories in the newspapers and magazines. This is not to omit the impact of the Web or the Internet on medical care and treatment. Thousands of patients, exasperated with the assembly-line pace of managed care, are turning to America's Doctor (americasdoctor.com), as well as such sites as CyberDocs (cyberdocs.org) ("Where the doctor is always in") and Web M.D. (webmd.com). To cite just one example, a Pennsylvania gynecologist works three shifts a week for America's Doctor, an online medical clinic that receives five hundred thousand visitors a month. As of now it's unclear how such cyberspace clinics will manage since state laws prohibit doctors from practicing in states where they are not licensed. But the truth is that cyberspace is the here and now of medicine and will most certainly grow in the future.

To some extent this is just a small taste of things to come. Big business and industry have plunged into the act as well. With health-care costs now in excess of $1.4 trillion a year and shooting upward each year, companies have a huge stake in controlling spiraling health-care costs.

In fact, if companies do not take action, they could see their profits wiped out within the next few years if health-care costs continue to rise. As a result, many companies have hired doctors to review the validity of employee health-care claims. They are also requiring second opinions. Some are increasing outpatient coverage in an effort to reduce hospital stays and offering incentives for employees to be cautious with the health-care dollar.

And to complicate matters even further, the sixties saw big business in the form of not-for-profit holding corporations enter health care even more. It started with nursing homes, and corporations have become so involved with them that today it is estimated that more than 50 percent of all nursing homes are owned by conglomerates or corporations.

The seventies saw the entrance of for-profit businesses into the hospital field. Through cost efficiencies and better screening of patients, larger hospitals have in many cases been able to show profits, while many of the smaller hospitals increasingly have felt the pinch and have gone out of business.

There also has been a trend by many, if not most, hospitals to acquire nursing homes, rehabilitation centers, surgicenters, or ambulatory care centers, sometimes in direct competition with doctors.

In addition, many physicians are feeling the pinch of competition stemming from other health-care professionals—nutritionists, stress counselors, and especially chiropractors, all of whom fall under the category of alternative health care. But as has already been noted, a rapidly growing number of physicians are using alternative medicine in cases where mainstream medicine is too costly or not called for.

Currently chiropractors, though unable to prescribe medicine or perform surgery, have seen a quadrupling of graduates in recent years, and as a group their median age is thirty-seven. What's more, chiropractors are now covered by Medicare and Medicaid, so doctors can look for more competition from this group.

SO WHERE DOES MEDICINE STAND?

Out of this hash of conflicting trends affecting medicine, where do we stand? There are factors that would seem to create a demand for physicians and others that would seem to lessen this demand.

We have noted factors that would seem to create a demand for generalists or primary care physicians and for a brake on specialists. The medical specialties that are expected to grow in personnel in the near future are those in the primary care area—general practice, internal medicine, pediatrics, obstetrics-gynecology, and geriatrics. Those expected to show surpluses are cardiology, gastroenterology, and anesthesiology. Much smaller increases in personnel requirements are foreseen for surgery and surgical subspecialties, psychiatry, and pathology.

In response to anticipated severe shortages in the number of physicians needed, Congress in 1963 passed legislation expanding the size and number of medical schools. The number of M.D.-dominated medical schools grew from eighty-nine to the present one hundred twenty-four and osteopathic medical schools rose from eight to sixteen. This enabled medical schools to nearly double the number of graduates by 1980 and likewise to double the number of graduates in practice. As noted in Chapter 1, the number of applicants per school opening dropped from 2.8 in the mid-1970s to 1.6 in 1988, but it rose again to 2.6 in 1994–1995. And further, the Council on Graduate Medical Education sees a surplus of 115,000 specialists in cardiology, gastroenterology, infectious diseases, endocrinology, pulmonary medicine, and several others.

But even with these predictions of surplus doctors in certain areas of medicine, there are literally thousands of communities across the United States and Canada that are very much underserved. In many smaller communities there are no physicians at all, and residents have to travel dozens of miles to reach the closest physician.

However, it is for this very willingness to serve the needs of small towns and rural areas that osteopathic medicine has registered such great gains in both membership and influence in recent years. And it is likewise for its unwillingness to settle in smaller communities that some observers have criticized mainstream medicine.

Others have pinned their hopes of correcting current imbalances in both the pay structure and number of physicians to such a system as the RBRVS.

As Walter Benjamin commented in an editorial in the *New England Journal of Medicine*, "Finesse of scalpel, catheter and CT scan is not superior but complementary to the diagnostic and pharmacological brilliance of the generalist. One form of medical artistry is learned by standing for hours at the surgical table; another form, learned from experience."

With some members of the profession earning $500,000 and more per year, while primary care doctors may make only $120,000 a year with the same amount of schooling, residency, and experience, clearly something is wrong.

Benjamin also criticizes the profession for creating a situation in which 25 percent of all practitioners list some form of surgery as their specialty but only 8 percent are in general or family practice. His solution is the immediate enactment of RBRVS to help remove these differences.

C H A P T E R 9

CONVERSATIONS WITH MEDICAL PROFESSIONALS

This chapter contains interviews with professionals and students involved in medicine. It will give you a clearer take on what is involved in pursuing a medical career.

THIRD-YEAR RESIDENT IN UROLOGY AT A LARGE PRIVATE HOSPITAL

I'm from Evanston, a suburb just north of Chicago. I did my undergraduate work at Indiana University in Bloomington, where I was contemplating going into business administration. But after a lot of thinking, I decided to go into medicine and was accepted by one of the large schools in Chicago. And after completing my medical school studies, I was accepted for a residency in urology. We offer one residency in urology every year.

After completing my coursework at Indiana University, I went to school at night—to Northwestern, where they have a night program in business. I should have given more thought about entering medicine before reaching this point, but I didn't, and I finally decided that the business world was not really for me. To me, it seemed to be a little bit like a shell game without really knowing if you would do well in this career without really doing anything for anyone but yourself.

So I finally made the decision to go to Rush, where I completed my studies in medicine, and now I'm in the third year of a five-year residency in urology. I chose Rush because I wanted to stay in the Chicago area and I had heard good things about it from people that I know who had gone there. I did have a good grade point average when I got into medical school—it was about 3.7.

Fortunately, I did not find medical school as tough as many claim that it would be, especially in the first two basic science years. It sort of suited by abilities. For one, I am good at memorization and the first couple of years is a lot of memorization. The second two years—the clinical years—were much more different than I expected. I guess I didn't have a very clear idea of what these would be like. I don't have anyone in medicine in my family. But I began to realize that a lot of medicine is like algorithmics, where you follow certain protocols and pathways, and it does not involve as much creative thinking as you might think.

The clinical years of medical school were definitely more interesting. The first two years you think you know everything. You take your classes, do well on the tests, and figure there's nothing you don't know. And then you get into your clinical years, and you quickly realize how little you do know because everyone tells you how little you know. But at the same time you realize how nothing is really black-and-white, and you begin to understand that the nature of medicine and the application of medicine are so much more of a gray area than you ever thought.

I chose urology because I wanted to do something surgical and it seemed to suit my personality. Surgery is somewhat of a hands-on kind of medicine. It's a sort of what can we do and what can't we do kind of medicine. True, it involves a lot of diagnostic work, but again in a lot of medicine—like in internal medicine, for instance, there's a lot more theorizing and a lot of it does not have much of a practical implication or any sort of therapeutics that you can apply. Whereas in surgery we tend to be very practically oriented. You tend to think there's a lot of things that you could figure out that will help you reach any diagnosis or treat somebody than you could otherwise.

So, the urology residency is typically five years, although some are six years because they include a year of research. At Rush we award one residency a year, and the first year, or intern year, you spend on general surgery rotations—so they are not really part of the urology residency. We have four residents who are actively participating in the urology service.

When I complete my residency, I'll probably go an academic route. I plan to do a urological oncology fellowship. I'll specialize in the cancer aspects of urology. You run into cancer in urology to a certain extent all of the time, unless you are very concentrated on infertility or erectile dysfunction. But the vast majority of urologists do deal with cancer regularly. The more complicated cases of cancer are often referred to the academic centers. So for the oncological subspecialty of urology you need one or more years of additional training. Some are more clinically oriented where you are in the operating room most of the time; others are two years where you spend a year in the laboratory. I would prefer to do one year of clinical work because that's where my interests really lie to handle the more complicated cases, but I may decide to do one lab year as well.

We residents do a lot of teaching of medical students, but they do not do much hands-on work, which is pretty much the case for all medical students. Most of the students who come through here are in surgery, but they must do some other kind of clinical surgery besides general surgery.

Urology has the reputation of having people in the field who are a little less imperialistic or intense than, say, general surgeons. They have a reputation of being a little more laid-back. We tell them that no matter what part of surgery they go into, they will probably have to deal with some patients with urological problems of some sort—patients who are having difficulty urinating or who have blood in their urine, and by rotating through our service they run into urological conditions that are pretty commonplace throughout the hospital.

In urology, we treat both men and women. There is some overlap between urology and gynecology—that overlap lies in the fact that we treat the kidneys and bladders and urethras of male and female patients. But as to external genitalia, we deal with men and in women external genitalia is pretty much the province of the gynecologist. But in the case of females who have frequency of urination or incontinence, that's something that both urologists and gynecologists handle.

The thing about urology is this: unlike surgeons who treat everybody surgically, in urology we treat many patients medically by prescribing medication that can clear up the problem—not every patient needs surgery.

It's true that all residents work an average of eighty hours a week, but it affects the residents in surgery more directly, and I think that most specialties are good at adhering to these hours. But it does require trade-offs, and I think that it has to be this way because the penalties for abusing residents' hours are pretty severe. So as a resident in urology I'm averaging seventy hours a week, and even though I'm on call every third day, I don't necessarily have to be in the hospital, as long as I'm available if needed or close enough to be on duty in fifteen to thirty minutes.

VETERAN UROLOGIST AND ASSOCIATE PROFESSOR OF UROLOGY AT A LARGE PRIVATE MEDICAL SCHOOL

I went to the University of Colorado in Boulder and finished there in 1980, and then I went to Tufts in New England Medical Center in Boston, where I did two years of general surgery.

How did I get into medicine? Well, that's quite a story. Neither of my parents went to college, but my dad's brothers all went to Harvard. And one of my uncles was a very famous doctor. He was the first doctor to actually diagnose FDR with polio, and he was one of the consulting physicians for President Eisenhower when he had his heart attack, so he was a very big man in medicine.

I probably saw him about six times in all, mostly when I was a child because he passed away before my bar mitzvah. So I don't remember him very well, but he had a great influence on me because my family spoke of him often and he was enormously respected. Another of my dad's brothers was a well-known cardiologist. When I was in my early teens, I decided that medicine was very appealing to me.

I decided to go into urology somewhat through the process of elimination. Nowadays, there is a very definite push to put medical students into primary practice, but when I was in medical school that was just starting to happen. At the University of Colorado, they had a strong family practice program. I enjoyed every field of medicine that I took in my four years of school. Each segment was interesting to me—pediatrics, general internal medicine, cardiology, surgery, even psychiatry appealed. I liked urology because it had the biggest opportunity to see patients of every age with a very broad spectrum of disease, from kidney stones and cancer to fertility problems and so forth.

It was also challenging in that I would be responsible for making the diagnosis. In many cases, surgeons have the patient presented to them by the internist, all ready to go—perhaps the patient has a gallbladder problem, and all the surgeon has to do is take it out. Or the patient has a heart problem—so fix it. In urology, you are more responsible for your own diagnosis, and this presented more of an intellectual challenge to me.

In urology you have more association with patients than most surgeons. And then too, I think that many of the problems in urology were not altogether worked out. The way I feel toward surgery is that surgery is a primitive therapy for a complex disease. As we get better with our diagnosis and better with our treatment, we're going to find fewer and fewer surgeries necessary. It's already happening. When I started out in urology in the eighties, one of the biggest areas of concern was kidney stone disease. Now we have this lithotripter that crumbles the stones mechanically and thus enables the body to get rid of them. So in some areas we have made great progress, and as we get to understand the disease better we can use less invasive, less injurious approaches to our treatment of disease.

As to my family and personal life, I'm married and have two daughters—ten and seven. There are several ways of looking at how medicine has affected my personal relationship with my family. If you look at it one way—it has compromised my personal life enormously. I don't have the same kind of daily interactions with my daughters as my friends. I'm at home for dinner once a week, and three weekends a month I'm in the office. Besides my clinical duties, I write for various medical journals and do research. This consumes what little time I have left when I am not taking care of patients.

But from my viewpoint as a physician, I find that I have no choice. It's what I want to do: to be at my best in my clinical practice so as to be able to make a contribution to medical science and to get my own personal satisfaction. This is the sacrifice that I have made to get these kinds of things.

I put in between sixty to eighty hours a week in my professional activities. Whatever free time I have, I am reading my journals or writing articles for them. I attend between three and five major medical meetings a year, and in three out of the five I also will be presenting papers.

After finishing my training, I spent five years at the University of Chicago Medical Center, where I was assistant professor of surgery and director of education for the department of surgery—including all surgery and surgery specialties.

At Rush, I am associate professor of urology and codirector of education for the department of urology. I am also involved in our residency program, where we train three or four young doctors a year. We are responsible for all training, including teaching during surgery and giving a regular lecture series. We work more on a clinical basis rather than in the classroom, and we are more involved with the care of the patients.

In summation then, if science turns you on, if service to people turns you on, if you like the intimacy and privilege of being able to take care of people—then you should consider a medical career. The idea of making it rich, being in a sense a very powerful person in the community—this status is rapidly changing today. If you are interested in the complexity of medical problems, then this is something that you should do. The other thing that's fascinating about medicine is that almost everything becomes routine in life, but in medicine you are always on a learning course. If you thrive on that idea of learning all the time, then medicine will be a very satisfying lifestyle.

PROFESSOR OF MEDICINE AND DIRECTOR OF CLINICAL PHARMACOLOGY

I didn't intend to go into clinical pharmacology. It was such a new discipline, and programs generally were not available in this area when I was in medical school.

I had always been interested in chemistry, physiology, and pharmacology in particular. As a senior medical student, I had taken elective research work in pharmacology, although I didn't have a clear idea of even doing research at the time. I finished Cornell School of Medicine in 1993 and have a degree in chemistry from Harvard, where I did my undergraduate work.

I went two years into a house staff training internship and residency at Massachusetts General Hospital during Vietnam and had to do my military service before I could continue house staff training, so I went to the National Institutes of Health for two years during the war. And it was there that I became interested in clinical research, while at the National Institute for Allergy and Infectious Disease. There I worked on a number of infectious diseases including leprosystematic mycoses (fungal diseases). It was there that I began doing what is now recognized as clinical pharmacology—during the years 1965 to 1967.

After another year of medical training, I came to Northwestern as chief medical resident in 1968. People at Northwestern suggested that I get more training in clinical pharmacology and then asked me to start the program there in 1970.

It is now a medical subspecialty, and there are several areas of concentration. You can do drug abuse and drug testing, or you can focus on therapeutic drugs and drug therapy for patients, and finally, you can do a tertiary care specialty for a research and teaching center.

Here in medical school, I run the drug assay lab for the hospital and for physicians, advising them on drug therapeutic problems. So, aside from patient research, I don't do primary clinical practice.

Obviously, if physicians ask me a question, I am available to help them—for instance, if a patient who is having trouble with the anticonvulsant drug Dilantin, which can cause problems, and the physician wonders why the patient is not recovering as well as expected. The blood level recorded may seem unusual in view of the dosage prescribed, so I might be asked to advise the physician on that. I would then give the patient a special test to see if there is something going on or how the drug is binding to proteins in the patient's blood.

When I started here there were no labs of this type in American hospitals. Mine was the first lab ever set up to apply research chemical techniques to the daily care of patients, and this has really developed over the past twenty-one years. I also function as the hospital quality control person and chair the pharmacy and the drug therapeutics departments, which decide about drugs to be carried in the patient pharmacy, as well as a committee that investigates adverse events that may occur to patients.

When working at the National Institutes of Health in clinical pharmacology, I was doing what today would be called clinical pharmacology, but at the time was thought of as infectious diseases. I was encouraged by the fact that my training as an undergraduate student in mathematics, chemistry, and physics could be applied to help patients and answer what I thought were clinically important problems.

My particular field is understaffed throughout the country. Not every medical school has a program in clinical pharmacology. Out of the present one hundred twenty-five schools, probably only thirty to forty have programs even in name—there are only about ten schools that have training programs in clinical pharmacology, which are funded by the NIH, so that anyone finishing the program can have various job opportunities in academic medicine or in the pharmaceutical industry, or even with the government. In the FDA (Food and Drug Administration), the agency desperately needs people with this kind of training.

We might be called on to work with a company to look at a new drug, or sometimes we are interested in certain drugs. We've actually gone to companies, and there is a breakdown product of protein or existing drugs, so we have actually initiated studies both in animals and humans of that particular drug.

We might consider hiring a company to look at the new drugs on the market, or sometimes we are interested in certain specific drugs. So we have actually initiated studies in the area.

In my work, I may refer to the mathematics of how drugs are distributed in the body and how they are eliminated. I probably spend about half my time on research and about a quarter in teaching. I teach about 10 percent of the second-year students a course in pharmacology and about a quarter of my time is spent on administrative work.

The department includes four faculty members besides me. Most have had special training beyond that of the conventional specialty—be that obstetrics, cardiology, or oncology, but they have a secondary specialty in clinical pharmacology.

One of our doctors is training in ob-gyn and in clinical pharmacology. Recently, she was in the news for her efforts on a low-birth-weight baby. She was part of a team who made the baby's birth possible. Her major research specialty is the organization of drug therapy in pregnant women. Many pregnant women have asthma and have to take theophylline. Our doctor has become expert in the changes that occur in pregnancy that would necessitate a change in the drug dose for such women.

Generally, the residents who do best in our program have had undergraduate training in chemistry and will have at least two years of calculus. Some may even have an engineering background in college, but must be really interested in research. All too often we find that many young people have good ideas for research but lack the dedication that is required and are unwilling to apply themselves to come up with the answer.

Beyond chemistry and calculus, we do not necessarily require an M.D. degree. We have a Ph.D. biochemist in our department who is expert in analysis and synthetic chemistry. It just doesn't make any sense to apply mathematics to drug therapy if you don't have good measurements of the drug or if you don't know what compounds are being converted to in the body—so we need that kind of expertise as well.

Clinical pharmacology is a subspecialty of internal medicine, anesthesiology, and psychiatry. The main binding element is that researchers have a special interest in using drugs scientifically.

This year we are offering our first certifying examination in clinical pharmacology, and requirements are that you must have had training in a primary subspecialty and additional training in clinical pharmacology. You can then get a certificate of competence. If you are a Ph.D., you could have training in primary care and two years of clinical pharmacology, so you could do it in five years altogether beyond medical school.

With regard to large companies like Abbott or Searle, most often I would function as a consultant to them. There are in addition several drug companies that will send their staff to sit in for a month or six weeks in an advanced course that we teach every fall in this area. So I am not doing any actual work for drug companies but am advising them as to how to set up their respective programs in clinical pharmacology.

In the future, I believe that what is happening in the automobile industry in quality control will be happening in medicine as well. And the clinical pharmacologist is in the best position to help monitor the quality of the drug usage. I have been choosing a committee for the Joint Commission on Accreditation of Healthcare Organizations, which certifies forty-five hundred hospitals and health-care organizations every year in a program that is called the Design for Living. Through this program, the Joint Commission is trying to improve the quality of drug utilization in health-care organizations—that is, by using the right drug at the right time and in the right dosage. Many of the things that have been part of the research techniques in clinical pharmacology are such a part of the expectations for optimum clinical care that they are being woven into the fabric of day-to-day patient care.

There is an opportunity for the clinical pharmacologist to play a leadership role in trying to develop ways to monitor usage—developing so-called indicators or guidelines that the Joint Commission can review as the basis for determining if the hospital is using drugs effectively.

ATTENDING ANESTHESIOLOGIST AND DIRECTOR OF OBSTETRICAL ANESTHESIA

Prior to joining the staff at Illinois Masonic Medical Center in Chicago, I was an attending anesthesiologist and director of obstetrical anesthesia with the Michael Reese Medical Center (1972 to 1974) and had a teaching appointment at the University of Chicago.

I did my medical training at the University of Illinois in Chicago. I became interested in medicine largely as a result of my high school biology

course and through the study of anatomy and physiology and zoology—
that was the biggest reason for my choice of medicine, a choice I made
when I was fifteen, and working in a drugstore after school, which whet-
ted my appetite.

At one time I even considered being a pharmacist, which was somewhat
related to medicine, but changed my mind. I got interested in anesthesiology during the first-year internship in internal medicine doing a rotation
in anesthesiology, which seemed to offer experience in dealing with acute
medicine and also seeing the immediate results of drugs and their
responses.

This is a very open field for qualified students, and there is not the back-
log of applications that you see in various surgical specialties, many of
which are hard to get into, such as ophthalmology, ENT, neurosurgery, and
plastic surgery.

I also am very much involved in training students (a clinical professor
of anesthesiology) and hold various other positions in the department, such
as training anesthesia residents and in a program approved by the ACGME
(Accrediting Council for Graduate Medical Education), which is a branch
of the AMA and the AAMC. With approved freestanding residencies here,
I hold various positions: one as chair of the resident selection committee
and another as chair of the clinical competence committee, which evaluates residents. I also am a member of the curriculum committee, vice-
chairman of the department, director of quality assurance, and of the
medical school committee, which includes the senior medical school electives subcommittee. Committee work never seems to stop; neither does my
work in medical societies and in anesthesia societies.

Anesthesia is unique in that teaching and clinical work in resident-
teaching programs are the same. I may be supervising one of two rooms
in the operating room. If there is an anesthesia obstetrics case scheduled,
there will be another attending to relieve me, and then I could cover the
anesthesia ob case with a resident-in-training. So most of the time I am
working, I am also teaching. On-the-job training is really clinical teaching. Right in the operating room, things are happening as medical students
rotate through the department.

We get medical students in one of two ways: those who are going
through their clinical rotations in the third year of medical school and
spend a week or two in anesthesiology as if it were a part of a surgical sub-

specialty. Or if they are taking a senior medical student elective in anesthesiology, we get students who are not specifically attached to a surgery clerkship. Usually this type of elective lasts four weeks and is a more intensive experience. The student may not be totally committed to anesthesiology but feels that it would be a good way to spend four weeks.

As to what it takes to succeed in anesthesiology, in many ways anesthesiology is no different from any other specialty. We look for the same kind of students. It would be good to have bright individuals who score well on exams. They are always welcome. They should also be comfortable in an emergency situation, emotionally mature, and like doing things with their hands. Last, but not least, they should be reasonably self-confident. Occasionally, we get some who can't fit these standards. Some may leave the field on their own; others have to be dropped. Still others may enter through medical specialties for various reasons. They may not have been happy where they were. Medicine gives you considerable flexibility to change your field on the specialty level. In other words, once you complete the basic training, there is a lot of latitude in medicine so that you can change your specialty at the postgraduate level. It is possible to get a new lease on life without incurring a lot in terms of years of training involved.

The benefits of anesthesiology are excellent. If you like to see immediate results of what you do rather than deal with chronic conditions, or if you like to practice medicine, acute physiology, and acute pharmacology, where you see immediate results from what you do, then this is the field for you, as opposed to internal medicine, let's say, where conditions can be chronic and one needs to have a lot more patience and follow patients for weeks and weeks on end before seeing any results.

An advantage and a drawback is that patient contact is limited. Usually, you see patients before anesthetic is administered and after recovery. Most of your contact verbally or with other people is with other personnel or workers. My contact on a daily basis is with other personnel, either in the operating room with surgeons, nurses, and residents, or with medical students. So I deal a lot in collegial relationships with other people who are connected to my work rather than with patients per se, although how one approaches patients and how one talks with them before they are anesthetized are also very important.

One other thing, anesthesiology is traditionally a high-risk profession. When you are a doing kind of a doctor, people can get hurt. I am making a distinction between thinking doctors and doing doctors. It's not that there are no cognitive efforts involved. There are, but we become more and more procedurally oriented. It's a numbers game, and the more procedures you do, the greater the likelihood of someone getting hurt or being unhappy about the results of the procedure. Now because of improvements in safety and technology, we are no longer in the high-risk category. The malpractice insurance carrier now says that the most risky subspecialties in terms of getting sued and in terms of cash payout are such fields as neurosurgery, obstetrics and gynecology, plastic surgery, and orthopedic surgery. These are the highest-risk specialties in terms of what you must pay for malpractice coverage. According to the American Medical Association, annual malpractice insurance premiums averaged $16,700 per physician in 1995.

As to hours, my twenty-four-hour in-house call happens once a week. This is pretty typical of the entire field, but in academic anesthesiology we get called less. You could be on call once in fourteen days in a large teaching medical center—once a month would probably be more typical. As long as you are not working late in the operating room, you are home free. So there is a big advantage in that there are no office obligations after hours. Once you're through with the operating room, usually you will not be bothered with phone calls.

Sometimes anesthesiologists are also involved in pain clinics or non–operating room duties. If you are involved with pain clinic kinds of patients, you could be a primary care physician for some patient. I know of one prominent anesthesiologist who was originally a surgical resident and who then contracted polio and lost the use of his legs and had to work from a wheelchair. He was then weaned from surgery to anesthesiology, which he was able to handle from a wheelchair, and he became interested in nerve blocking and was very prominent in academic anesthesiology. Painkilling is one area where anesthesiologists have gotten away from a passive role in patient care to a more active role like that of the primary care physician. Blocks in the operating room and nerve blocks could be both diagnostic and therapeutic depending on the reason they were given. Some anesthesiologists are also involved in acupuncture and transcutaneous electrical stimulation. Pain clinics tend to be multimodal in what they offer. They can offer physical therapy and even manipulation that sounds like a chiropractor. In other words, they must know what spinal manipulation involves. So pain clinics tend to be much more eclectic. They can involve physical therapy and nerve injections and blocks as well as the aforementioned manipulation.

I attended Washington University in St. Louis as an undergraduate and Rush Medical College in Chicago as a medical student, where I remained for my internship and my residency in internal medicine.

In college I majored in psychology with the intention of going into medicine. I was premed from the start. I didn't major in science for two reasons: science courses are generally the hardest classes and I wanted to broaden my horizons.

In many colleges, biology, chemistry, and organic chemistry are very difficult, and when I was in college, grades were always paramount in being admitted to medical school. Although the schools will say that grades are not the only factor and that they look at your overall background, the fact remains that without the grades, regardless of extracurricular activities, you will have a hard time getting into medical school. So grades are a big factor that you can't get around. I suggest that if you concentrate on one science course at a time, you have a much better chance of getting an A in that course.

I didn't want to be a whiz at science only. It's a good idea to have knowledge in other areas and not be so focused that you have no peripheral vision. Besides, medical schools are looking for people who are well-rounded and have interests besides medicine.

I got into medicine basically for two reasons: for one, in school, biology seemed to be the subject of greatest interest to me. And in high school, I enjoyed working on projects involving the human body. I enjoyed biology and thought it was fun and was fascinated at how the body works. The other factor in choosing medicine was the fact that my father was a physician, so I was exposed to medicine at an early age, and this was certainly a factor in my choice. But it was not because I really liked some other field and said to myself, "Well, my dad is a doctor and I'll follow him." The fact of the matter is that I always have enjoyed biology, and I have always liked people, so medicine seemed to be a good way of combining these interests.

I always assumed that I would go into private practice like my dad had done, since that was what my exposure had been, and I was not sure I really had a broad enough vision of medicine to really understand all of my options. I probably did not experiment in enough areas to really get a good feeling of what my options were.

As to my choice of internal medicine, a lot of your feeling about this depends on the people that you work with and who you look up to. If you're in a hospital with a tremendous ob-gyn program and the people are terrific and great teachers, you will lean toward ob-gyn. If internal medicine happens to be the best specialty you have been exposed to, you lean toward it.

The experience obtained in your third-year rotations at medical school is a big factor, and you should try to get as much experience in these clinical rotations as you can before deciding on the field in which you wish to specialize. You don't have a lot of time, since you must apply for residencies at the beginning of your senior year.

Generally, my day has three components—hospital rounds, teaching, and office hours. Over the years my time investment in these areas has fluctuated, and I learned to invest my time in other areas for diversity of experience. For example, at first I did not just sit in the office and see patients eight hours a day, five or six days a week, I became a consultant for psychiatric patients, working with a substance abuse program at the hospital where I was training. I was one of the few interns in the area, so everyone was calling on me for consults, and I spent 30 percent of my time doing this. I became the medical school consultant for the creation of a videotape for continuing medical education on alcoholism. I was also teaching, and through some friends, I was introduced to a real-estate developer who builds retirement homes, and I was offered the opportunity to become medical director of a few of these homes. This began about eight years ago and lasted until about two years ago and was quite different from my private practice. So there are many different things going on in my career. Today I allocate 16 percent of my time to teaching, and the rest of my time is spent on my practice and hospital rounds.

It's important in medicine to be flexible because everything is changing—hospitals are opening and closing (primarily closing), there are fewer opportunities, and more people are looking for the chance to do the same thing.

It's unfortunate, but when we go through medical school and college, we focus too much on medicine and science. It would be worthwhile for anyone planning a career in medicine or research to have some sort of business education. Because as much as you would not want to think of it that way, running an office, practice, or health-care department is a business, and you get no business experience in medical school. You really should know something about accounting principles, overhead, insurance, personnel relations, and unemployment insurance. This is part of the reason so few medical school graduates are going into private practice but are joining groups instead. If I had known this, I probably would have done things differently.

I have a large number of geriatric patients because working for my dad for a number of years before he retired, I inherited a lot of patients that loved him, so automatically I had a lot of geriatric patients.

Second, the area in which I practice has a high percentage of geriatrics, so many of the new patients I see are also geriatric patients. So I took an examination to become certified in geriatrics as well as in internal medicine. However, I don't list myself as a gerontologist, because I really enjoy handling the younger patients in my practice, as well as the geriatric patients, who account for about 75 percent of my practice.

Private practice of internal medicine is one of the most difficult options in medicine for two reasons: first, you are basically on call all of the time, especially if you're a solo practitioner and you have responsibility for care twenty-four hours a day. You never know when you will have an emergency that you cannot foresee and schedule, so your patient load is unpredictable. And second, you are expected to be 100 percent accurate and available. I might add that you're the most underpaid of all the specialists because internal medicine is a cognitive skill and has never been paid on the level of procedural medicine. Patients and insurance companies are oriented toward paying for procedures. That is why applications for residencies in internal medicine have dropped 30 percent.

Today's graduates do not go into internal medicine anymore. They go into radiology, anesthesiology, ophthalmology, orthopedic surgery—into fields where they can get paid a lot for a small investment of time. When you consider that an eye doctor gets $2,000 for a cataract removal, which takes him forty-five minutes to do, and it takes the internist five or six days of work to make that much money—it's not very equitable. So many people who go into medicine go into areas involving procedures rather than going into private practice. Who can blame them. I can sit in my office and make $60 an hour, and someone in a subspecialty can do one procedure for $500 in twenty minutes. And that's why Medicare is now seeking to see how the system works. There will always be a discrepancy in how doctors are paid—procedures will always be paid more than cognitive functions. There will be some narrowing of the gap, but it will not be dramatic and will not catch up and equalize.

As to private practice, today instead of having patients who pay you and write a check at the time of the service, you must deal with HMOs and PPOs, and you have Medicare and commercial insurance, and every company has its own requirements for payment. Some require that you call the insurance carrier before you hospitalize someone; you must have authorization.

Liability insurance certainly detracts from our profitability. We are constantly making sure that we are covering ourselves. I know a urologist who is also a lawyer. If I send a patient to this doctor, no matter what the problems, the patient will get a complete workup. Most urologists will say that they don't believe it's worth proceeding at this point with all of these tests, but some feel it isn't worth the legal risk not to.

If I have somebody with a severe headache and don't do a CT scan, I am liable if there's a brain tumor. And yet, more and more insurance companies won't let you test unless you have a good reason, and a severe headache is not sufficient enough to proceed. So the insurance company tries to limit testing, but fear of malpractice makes it obligatory. Now if I have someone in the hospital with a bad heart, I will call in a cardiologist to cover myself. If that patient has a complication, even though the cardiologist has not changed anything that I do, I can say that I have a cardiologist on the case and the cardiologist has agreed that this is what I have to do. So the doctor has a lot of extra expense because of liability. Our insurance premiums go up, which can account for 15 percent of our income. So it's a constant problem that goes back to the need to be perfect all of the time and not miss anything, cover yourself, and make sure that you're not liable and cannot be sued for anything.

At the same time there is a lot of positive feedback in medicine when you help save people's lives or make them feel better. There is a lot of gratification in the work. I see people who are commodity brokers, and their net worth in life is based on the numbers on the board at the end of the day. It's the old feeling of, "See, I'm better than you because I made $50,000 and you've only made $30,000." That's why a lot of them go into charity work to make their lives more meaningful and fulfilling. I get fulfillment out of my practice, as well as aggravation.

Medicine is an excellent career, and there are many rewards. It is particularly rewarding if you enjoy working with people. If you like working with your hands and doing procedures, there's a lot of potential in medicine.

DIRECTOR OF ADMISSIONS AT A PRIVATE MEDICAL SCHOOL

This year we had about 8,702 applications, and we will interview about 650 and accept 220 for a class of 104 students. We accept more than we have room for because we know that some of those accepted will register in other schools. But of the 8,700 who apply, only about 4,500 complete the application and go through the entire application process.

Most students will have applied to twelve to fifteen schools and have multiple acceptances. It's not so much a matter of going for numbers. You could apply to 100 schools, and if they are the wrong schools, you still might not get in.

This year is again a peak year. The expectation is that applicants will begin to decrease within the next few years, but at this point we continue to see an increase like never before—this was a record number of applications for us.

I might point out that it's not just the students with top scholastic records that we accept. That would be an easy job if all we were interested in were the numbers.

In evaluating the backgrounds of students, we take into consideration their scholastic grade point average, their MCAT, and their motivation—they are all pieces of the puzzle and must all be there. They have to be able to show that they can academically and interpersonally manage the demands of medical school, and they have to demonstrate that they know why they want to go to medical school. If any of these pieces is missing, then they're not a candidate for admission.

In terms of the increased number of applicants, there are people applying now who did not really have that option before. One large group is women. There are more female applicants now than ever before. We accept slightly more than 40 percent women, which is fairly typical of what's happening in all medical schools.

Students who see a professional career as a way to security are choosing medicine in larger numbers, while fewer students are choosing law school, business school, or engineering.

And I see students who have a greater commitment to service than in previous years—even five years ago. There are more students who are going into medicine because it's the way that they want to serve their fellow man. They seem to have more of the luxury of being idealistic. It's an exciting trend.

We are working very hard to increase the number of students from underrepresented backgrounds. We regularly talk to high school groups. Last year we admitted about 3 percent underrepresented in minorities—primarily African-Americans but also including Puerto Ricans, Native Americans, Alaskans, and Chicanos.

The school receives in the mail the American Medical College Association Service common application, which has biographical data and information on activities in school and out, both college-related and outside of the university. It contains a personal essay in which they can write anything they want. The application also contains biographical information and detailed information on grade point average broken down several ways—for the sciences, the nonsciences, all courses, and each year of undergraduate college. There also is an indication of scores on the standardized exams. All schools that you apply to receive a copy of this.

Most schools require a supplementary application, and we are one of these schools. Students start to apply for admission on June 15, which is the earliest they can. By the end of July, we will have received about 400 applications, and by the end of the application process, which is December 15, we will receive 5,400 applications for 104 spaces.

Each application is then assigned to the committee members for schools in that area, who review the application and decide if the person should be invited in for an interview, rejected, or placed on hold for later review after seeing what the applicant pool looks like.

If the faculty member's decision is to interview, the student is invited for an interview at his or her convenience. Some schools will assign a date but are flexible and will reschedule if it's not convenient for the student, or they may tell the student to come in any given period, say between now and the next few weeks. Usually they come in for three interviews: one with someone on the committee, usually with the person that suggested that they come in for an interview; one with a faculty member at large; and the last with a student. We give them an orientation to the school, which either I or the dean of students handles, a talk by the financial aid officer, who discusses financing a medical education, and a senior medical student will talk to them about life at our school. They may go to lunch with a freshman or sophomore medical student, students who are about the same age as the applicant, and they tour the medical center. Altogether, they will spend about a day on all phases of the interview and orientation. Most other schools do about the same. Some schools give one interview only, others two, and still others give three. At some schools, only the admissions committee does the interviewing, and at others this is handled by the faculty at large.

After the interview, the interviewer fills out a report and faculty members write their comments. When all comments are back, the person who first recommended the interview presents the application with all of the comments, and the committee votes to accept, reject, or hold the application for future decision.

What do we look for in a student? We look at the whole application. We have certain averages to be sure, but are more concerned with the overall student. True, the average acceptable grade is 3.65, and for the MCAT, it is about 11. But we accept some students whose grade point is below average but falls somewhere in the range of 3.0 to 4.0 and an MCAT that is below 11, or part above average and part below average. But they may show an improvement in grades, and thus show that they can do the work.

This is also true of their MCAT scores—there may be some very good reason why they did not do well on some part of the MCAT. This is especially true of recent immigrant students who usually have very low reading scores. They are not necessarily poor readers, but read more slowly. They may have super grades in every other area of the test, but average only 4 in the reading instead of the average 8 for other students. We're willing to allow and accept that.

Next, we look at the letters of recommendation that come from the professors. They may say that the kid has grades that are not terribly impressive but that he or she is working twenty hours a week and is volunteering at the hospital throughout schooling and doing tutoring as well. These letters of recommendation are very important in helping us to understand the interpretation of students' course grades and test scores.

We then decide if the student is academically qualified and suitable for our school; in other words, a good fit. If the kid is from a rural background and wants to practice family medicine in Montana, this is not the best school for him. We produce the highest percentage of any medical school in the country—nearly 25 percent of every graduating class—who go full time into academics. So we have to consider who we are, what the student's undergraduate record and grade point average are, and we put certain students in jeopardy by admitting them here, no matter how great they are.

So we bring them in for an interview and try to determine their suitability from these personal talks. That is why we have somebody on the committee who has seen their record. We want to see what they are like as people and if they would fit in here and get an idea of their aptitude at self-expression, the depth of their thought processes as they handle ambiguous situations, their social skills, all kinds of things. I don't think there is any medical school in the country that would give up the interview. It's a valuable tool.

The number of women in medical school in the last twenty years has gone from about 8 percent of the total class to a little more than 40 percent. And this is a national trend.

There is no strong sentiment to increase or decrease the number of medical students. About sixteen thousand medical students enter medical school. Fortunately, our attrition rate is low—only about 1 percent—and this is true nationwide. Attrition often involves kids who are pushed into medicine. They get here, clear the hurdle of entry into school, and they die. It's really sad to see.

DEAN OF STUDENTS AND CHIEF FINANCIAL OFFICER

The thing I usually tell students is that financing their education is as important as finding out about the curriculum of the medical school. As they begin the process, they should write and ask for a financial aid pamphlet. This will help them to gain the information they need to get their questions on finances answered if they are invited to the school for an interview.

Obviously, the schools are divided between public and private and depending on the state in which the student lives—for instance, in Chicago, we only have six medical schools—one public and the rest private. So if you say your home school or home state will provide you advantages, that may or may not be true, but generally speaking, public schools are going to cost less to attend.

Also there is a movement afoot because the competition for places in medical school is so strong right now, there are three applicants for every place. And so what the students are doing is casting a broader net to seek out enough applications in hopes of being considered. So if a student applies to a state institution, but it's not in their home state, the cost of education in that institution is almost as much as in a private school.

And in fact the student will sometimes find that given the financial aid packages available at private institutions, it costs them only a small amount more to attend a private school than a public school. So looking at the school's resources now becomes critical.

Watch out if you go to an institution and they say to you, "Our student budget for this year is $46,000 and we have very limited resources to offer students—we have no loans available, and we have no scholarships available and we have none whatever of our own." But they do have access to all of those unsubsidized loan programs that are much more costly.

There are all kinds of private outfits out there that would like to loan to medical students—such as Med Access, Med Achiever, and Med Assist—everybody's got a program for the medical student. On paper, they'll loan the student on the same arrangement as some of the good loans, but what you need to know is that for every dollar you borrow on these programs, you're likely to repay three dollars.

And that's why when you say $50,000 debt, that doesn't sound too bad. But $50,000 of one of these loans where you're paying three times the amount for every dollar loaned is a lot different than $50,000 where you are only paying $1.27 for every dollar. So understanding what the school can do is critical.

The military has been the mainstay for the service commitment kind of medical program. They don't require that the student commit to any particular specialty. But the students are required to pay their military debt off first, and usually that's a year's service for every year that they participate in the program. They have programs where you can participate in the second or third year or the fourth year, but if you take it for one year, that's the minimum.

But it should be noted that there are limitations on the number of positions they can offer. And the student should understand that if they want to go to school where and when they want to, they probably should not do the military.

Now the second way of paying for your schooling in service is through the National Health Service Corps. And this agency, like many federal agencies, has also been under fire. There are real questions about, "Is it better to accept funding for medical school that you know that you will have to pay back, or is it better in the military, where for every year committed, you are going to give them back a year of service?" The National Health Service

Corps is restrictive in that you must be willing to commit to primary care. This is often problematic for some of the students when they come in because they don't know if primary care is what they want to do. It seems like now it's a recognized national need where there's a lot of pressure on the student to go into primary care.

But the question that the government is struggling with now with regard to the National Health Service Corps is if they want to put more funding in the physician repayment side because that way they are not funding an education for students who may or may not commit to what it is they need.

And there are also several programs for surgeons that are offered through the National Institutes of Health if you are interested in academic medicine. You work off your debt the same as the National Health Service program as a research scholar or at the NIH. And like the National Health Service program, you receive $22,000 a year for every year that you commit to. So those are very nice programs, but they are very restricted and there's a lot of competition for them.

Now one of the things that we ask of our seniors, after they finish school, concerning scholarships is, "Were you awarded a scholarship at any time during your four years from the Association of American Medical Colleges?" We have found that 60 percent of our students said that yes, they had some sort of a scholarship, as opposed to 39 percent who didn't (and the 1 percent who didn't respond).

So obviously it's important that you get all of this information on the programs and what they cost, what the options are, and if you want to give time in service for funds received or if you are interested in research. If you are borrowing money, which includes 60 to 70 percent of all medical students in the country, what you want to do is first take a look at that student budget, and there are ways you can do that. For one, you could get three roommates and share an apartment, and you can't afford to go to $7.50 movies to see a show; go to campus film showings at a fraction of the cost. You have to limit your calls home.

If they live like a physician while they're in medical school, they will live like a student when they are a physician. So it's their choice, and they need to know what they are doing.

Many of our students also work. Many feel that working is out of the question. But there are things that they can do. For instance, they can work as teaching assistants, which can net a student anywhere from $1,800 to $2,400 a quarter. Now that can really help meet budget costs. You've got to work for that money, but that money is yours and it doesn't come with a promissory note. So we encourage students to figure out ways to cut their costs and what they can do to earn some extra income. And then basically there are tons of outside scholarships that are available, but you have to look for them. You've got to go to the library and check all of the books that are out there on where to get financial aid, and then figure out any and all loans or funds that you might qualify for, and you should apply for these. Last year we had twenty to twenty-five students who were able to write away for scholarships for which they qualified, and this amounted to about $110,000 in outside scholarships alone. So being assertive and asking is absolutely critical.

But even so we are seeing a lot of indebtedness, much of it in the $100,000 or more category. Right now, this includes about 24 percent of our students. And within two or three years, we figure that it will be 40 percent in this category.

So what you've got to do is to begin to keep an eye on the marketplace, because there are lots of changes in this marketplace for physicians. There is a physician oversupply. They have to say to themselves, "Well, gee, I've always wanted to be a neurosurgeon, but the number of neurosurgeons is in tremendous oversupply." And physicians' incomes have been going down, but they are still good in comparison with a lot of other occupations. But there are some trade-offs that the student should realize.

Now through the Free Application for Federal Student Assistance, called the FAFSA, and because medical students are independent students, they can fill out their own personal information about what their earnings are, what their assets are, and this then is transmitted to the various places that do a needs analysis. That information is then transmitted to the schools, and the schools then can use that as the basis for awarding federal loan programs.

We tell students that if they want to borrow the $8,500 of subsidized Stafford and $10,000 of unsubsidized Stafford loans, then they can borrow money from the Perkins fund, if that's available. This can all be done as an independent student and not having to turn in other sources of information.

So that in a nutshell is the package for determining financial aid. You go to the school's financial aid office, they go through your own budget and make a determination of how much a student can contribute, and they look at need and what the school can provide through the various loan and scholarship funds to meet these needs, and that's what the student needs to know.

Then we can determine what the student is expected to contribute, what the parents are asked to contribute, and what the school can do in the way of loans and scholarships to meet their anticipated needs. Sometimes, if the parents are unable to provide the money that we say they should, we will refer the students to these more expensive alternative loan funds if the student is unwilling or unable to work to make up the difference.

There's all sorts of money out there to pay for a medical education. Get the best dollars you can so that the total indebtedness is not more than you can handle after you graduate.

C H A P T E R

THE SPECIALTIES AND SUBSPECIALTIES

In this chapter we will describe the twenty-four medical specialty areas and the sixty-six subspecialties accredited by the American Board of Medical Specialties as of 2004 (see Appendix B). But new specialties are constantly being developed, and there will most likely be several new recognized subspecialties by the end of the year. For more information about the training requirements for the various specialties and subspecialties, write to the appropriate certifying boards or specialty societies listed in Appendix B.

ALLERGY AND IMMUNOLOGY

Allergy and immunology, originally a subspecialty of pediatrics and internal medicine, received specialty status with the formation of the Board of Allergy and Immunology in 1972. These specialists are involved with the overreaction of the body's immune system to external stimulants or allergens. Ordinarily, such stimulants trigger desirable reactions to repel invaders such as pollen or dirt before they can enter the body, but some such reactions can result in pain and discomfort, and even danger. Take, for instance, a person who is allergic to penicillin. To most people, penicillin is a safe and effective way to block various infections, but to the person who is allergic to penicillin, this agent can produce some real problems—from welts on the hands and feet to a very dangerous reaction known as anaphylaxis, which results from an overproduction of antibodies to penicillin or other allergens.

Ordinarily, however, people suffering from allergy are treated for milder reactions to allergens, such as sneezing, sniffles, itchiness, and skin reactions including eczema and welts.

To treat the symptoms of allergy, the allergist tests the patient with a series of small doses of various substances, including a variety of foods and other allergens ranging from cat and dog dander to pollen, dust, and ragweed. If the patient shows positive reactions to any of these substances, the allergist administers a series of injections consisting of small doses of the substances to which the patient is allergic. In this way the patient builds up a gradual immunity to the substances in the same manner that a patient who is immunized to polio, smallpox, or diphtheria builds an immunity to those diseases.

Since treatment can last for years, the allergist may treat all continuing patients plus whatever new ones come in. Allergists are predominantly involved in clinical medicine, although some go into academic work or research. Because treatments can last years, allergists often form close relationships with their patients. And since, as often happens, members of the same family may share the same allergies, the doctor may treat several members of the same family in much the same manner as the family practitioner or internist.

Hours are fairly regular because most patients are healthy otherwise. But the wheezing associated with some allergic reactions, and asthma, can be dangerous. Such dangerous reactions can occur at any time, day or night.

In 2004, there were seventy-two officially accredited training programs in allergy and immunology, most of them running two years long and a few, three years, to accommodate those who want to do additional research or prepare for academic careers. This is in addition to a three-year residency in either internal medicine or pediatrics. There are in addition eleven programs in an accredited subspecialty, clinical and laboratory immunology.

ANESTHESIOLOGY

An anesthesiologist is trained to provide pain relief and maintenance during or immediately following an operation or an obstetric or diagnostic procedure. They work primarily behind the scenes in hospital operating rooms and emergency rooms administering anesthetics (drugs) to patients undergoing surgery or dental procedures and mothers-to-be in the delivery of their babies. The object, of course, is to make the procedure as pain free as possible. In most cases, the patient is completely under or oblivious to pain, although in many procedures the anesthetics are local or confined to a specific part of the body. In monitoring the delivery of anesthetics, the anesthesiologist often must make life-and-death decisions involving the patient's vital signs—pulse, blood pressure, and respiration—at a complex console used to control the input of anesthetic and to monitor its effect on the patient.

In many cases they diagnose and treat acute, long-term, and cancer pain problems as well as diagnose patients with critical illnesses or severe injuries. They also are called on to direct resuscitation in the case of patients with cardiac or respiratory emergencies, including the need for artificial ventilation. In addition, they supervise postanesthesia recovery.

To do this work the anesthesiologist must have a vast background in physiology and pharmacology. The hours are ordinarily fairly predictable, except for emergencies, which can arise at any time.

Patient contact ordinarily is limited to pre- and postsurgery visits, primarily to describe the procedure and thus to help relieve patient anxiety. The anesthesiologist must be able to react coolly and swiftly under stress and to adroitly manipulate a bag containing anesthetic or pure oxygen. Surgery procedures handled by the anesthesiologist range from simple tonsillectomies to complex open-heart surgery. Training involves a base year, or internship, followed by two three-year residencies in clinical anesthesiology and critical care. Approximately one hundred thirty-two programs are offered per year in anesthesiology, fifty in critical care medicine, and ninety-eight in pain medicine.

A few programs offer training in special areas of anesthesiology—pediatrics, obstetrics, and neurosurgery, which are often applied for separately from regular anesthesiology training programs. Long hours in addition to occasional overtime make this a somewhat stressful but well-paying field. In 2004, anesthesiologists averaged approximately $323,000 per year. Certification in the subspecialties of critical care medicine and in pain medicine require additional training and examination.

COLON AND RECTAL SURGERY

Formerly known as proctology in allopathic medicine, the name of this surgical specialty was changed to reflect the broader scope of the field. Specialists treat various diseases of the intestinal tract, colon, rectum, and both anal and perianal areas by surgical and medicinal means. Conditions commonly treated include polyps, inflammatory bowel disease, abscesses, fissures, colitis, and diverticulitis. Colon and rectal surgical specialists also are skilled in treatment and diagnosis of endoscopic procedures of the rectum and colon. Colon and rectal residency programs now offer training in minimally invasive abdominal surgery involving the colon and rectum.

Since patients are referred by primary care doctors, specialists in this field are located primarily in midsize to large cities. They spend a lot of their time in their offices and in the hospital, since emergencies are relatively few and hours are more regular than those of most physicians. One of the primary reasons students choose this field is that most conditions are relatively easy to diagnose and treat.

However, the training is among the lengthiest of all medical specialties, involving a five-year residency in general surgery followed by a one-year fellowship in colon and rectal surgery. Average gross yearly income for colon and rectal surgery was $329,000 in 2004, higher than general surgery, which was $291,000 a year.

As one of the smaller surgical specialties (with thirty-seven residency programs in 2004), there were far more applicants than programs. The field closest to colon and rectal surgery in osteopathy is proctology, which is more limited in scope and is different than what was formerly known as proctology in allopathic medicine.

DERMATOLOGY

The focus of the dermatologist is the diagnosis and treatment of pediatric and adult patients with benign and malignant (cancerous) disorders of the skin, mouth, external genitals, hair, and nails, as well as a number of sexually transmitted diseases. The field is vast, concentrating as it does on the skin, the covering that encases the entire body, including the vital organs, as a protective covering and houses many sensory nerves that serve as an early warning for such hazards as extreme heat or cold and other potentially dangerous agents.

Besides the dermatologist's need to understand the diseases that can affect the skin, this specialist has additional training in the diagnosis and treatment of contact dermatitis, as well as skin cancers, melanomas, moles, and other tumors of the skin, as well as allergic and nonallergic skin disorders. They must be able to cope with and understand the emotional turmoil that often accompanies such problems as eczema and acne. The latter is a particularly sensitive area for teenagers. Fortunately, since most skin conditions are readily apparent, most patients come to the dermatologist in the early stages when the disease is most easily treated.

One of the most serious conditions treated by the dermatologist is skin cancer, often unnoticed by the patient or his or her family in the early stages. However, except for a more serious form of cancer known as melanoma, most skin cancers are easily removed by surgery and cauterizing.

In the case of severe allergic reaction, the dermatologist may treat the symptoms of the disease that cause itchiness or scaly skin. Besides removal of skin tumors and cancer, the dermatologist also deals with warts and eczema.

To qualify for this profession, you must complete a four-year residency, including a first year in emergency medicine, family practice, general surgery, internal medicine, obstetrics and gynecology, or pediatrics.

Training programs, of which there are currently one hundred nine, are established by the Residency Review Committee for Dermatology and the American Board of Pathology. In addition, certification in subspecialties includes forty-four in clinical and laboratory dermatological immunology and dermatopathology as well as pediatric dermatology, which requires additional training and examination.

EMERGENCY MEDICINE

Emergency medicine became the twenty-third of the twenty-four accredited medical specialties in 1979 and currently numbers twenty-one thousand specialists who have completed its residency programs.

Basically emergency medicine physicians (or ER physicians as they are often called) work primarily in hospital emergency rooms and are trained to recognize, diagnose, and treat a wide variety of conditions and emergencies that present themselves. These can range from a marble lodged in the throat of a small child to treating victims of stabbings and those injured in auto accidents, who may have multiple fractures and massive internal bleeding.

ER physicians must be able to act coolly and swiftly under high pressure, such as the arrival of a number of patients each requiring quick and knowledgeable treatment. Since patients arrive at any hour, day or night, and cases can involve various medical and surgical procedures to stabilize the patient, hours can be quite lengthy. Seldom, however, do ER physicians receive calls outside of assigned working hours. But since the work is twenty-four hours a day, these specialists may be called on often to work schedules that involve late nights and weekends and that can change from day to day. This can be quite stressful to both the physician and to his or her family.

Because of the nature of the work, where ER physicians seldom have control over who comes through the emergency room door, rarely if ever are they able to form lasting relationships with patients. Instead, they must be prepared to care for and treat whoever comes in at any time.

Most of the one hundred thirty-two ER training programs are either three or four years long. In addition there are several combined training programs in internal medicine and pediatrics that involve five-year residencies. There are also subspecialty programs involving additional training and examination including medical toxicology (twenty programs); pediatric emergency service (eight programs); and sports medicine (three programs).

FAMILY PRACTICE

In 2005 the American Board of Family Practice changed its name to the American Board of Family Medicine, perhaps reflecting the broad scope of this medical specialty. Often regarded as the prototype of medicine prior to the onset of specialization, the family doctor, as he or she was then known, was what the general physician who practiced in the days prior to 1940 was most often called. At the time, such physicians comprised the vast majority of doctors then practicing, and as family doctors they treated a wide array of ailments and disorders ranging from measles and whooping cough to warts, minor cuts, abrasions, and fractures as well as a host of other medical problems, including the delivery of babies. Family practitioners, as they are called, became a certified branch of medicine in 1969.

Because of the wide range of diseases and ailments they see, family physicians must have a deep background in medical diagnostic, testing, and treatment techniques, as well as of drugs and how they are used most effectively.

With the proliferation of medical knowledge and therapeutics in recent decades, family physicians cannot be expert in all medical problems, but it is estimated that they can treat up to 90 percent of the cases that they see.

As is true of other primary care physicians—internists, pediatricians, and obstetrician-gynecologists—family physicians are gatekeepers and sources of referral to other medical specialists when such expertise is warranted.

In the past, family physicians were largely solo practitioners working primarily out of their own offices, but this is no longer true, with an estimated 40 percent of these doctors working in group practices while another 57 percent participate in alternative health programs such as HMOs, PPOs, and IPAs.

Like the field of medicine as a whole, family practice calls for infinite patience, tact, and understanding, as well as plenty of enthusiasm and sympathy in handling problems from ailments of tiny infants to diseases of the elderly.

While family physicians are trained to deliver babies, this is not often a part of family practice, primarily because of the difficulty and expense of obtaining liability (malpractice) insurance to cover this aspect of the practice.

With the income of family physicians about the lowest of all physicians, averaging about $135,000 in 2004, this explains, in part, the difficulty of attracting students to this field in the past. At the same time, hours are long, with the family physician devoting sixty-five hours a week to patient care. Approximately 60 percent of that time is spent in office visits, 13 percent in hospital rounds, 14 percent in other patient visits, and 4 percent in surgery.

Despite the long hours and the low salaries, family physicians get great satisfaction from following patients over many years and establishing close friendships with their patients. Because of the variety of ills treated the family physician receives a broad range of training encompassing internal medicine, pediatrics, obstetrics and gynecology, psychiatry, and geriatrics.

With additional training, the family physician can be certified for geriatrics and, as is true of emergency medicine, in the promotion of wellness and the prevention of disease in sports medicine.

Currently there are four hundred seventy-seven training programs for family physicians offered in hospitals and clinics throughout the United States and Canada. Subspecialty training programs include geriatric medicine (thirty programs) and sports medicine (sixty-three programs).

INTERNAL MEDICINE

With 147,000 active practitioners, internal medicine is by far the largest of all medical specialties and, with at least sixteen subspecialties, it might be called the granddaddy of medicine as well. Practitioners in subspecialties of internal medicine include cardiologists, gastroenterologists, and hematologists, who must first complete their training in internal medicine before they can qualify for any subspecialty.

In general internists, as these specialists are known, treat and diagnose a variety of acute and chronic ailments affecting the organs and the various body systems. In one day, the internist may see patients suffering from disorders ranging from diabetes, arthritis, flu, and colds to heart problems and infectious diseases.

They differ from family physicians in that their practice is limited primarily to adults, although it might include adolescents as well; they do not ordinarily deliver babies. The practice is as broad and varied as that of the family physician and calls for a background of like intensity.

Like family physicians, internists are at the beck and call of their patients, an aspect of the work that often intrudes on their personal lives and family ties. Internists also often develop close and satisfying ties with patients over many years.

Basically the field could be described as cognitive in that these specialists almost always are attempting to diagnose and treat the various ills affecting their patients. Thus the work involves the use of tests, the doctor's own observations and probing, the patient's medical history, and the particular ill or disorder involved.

Because of the emphasis on the cognitive, or diagnostic, aspect of medicine, internists are on the low end of the pay scale, averaging $176,000 in 2004. Interestingly, the earnings of many subspecialists are often much greater than those of internists. In such specialties as cardiology (cardiovascular medicine) and urology, doctors are often called on to do such procedures as angiography in the case of cardiologists and lithotripsy in the case of urologists, which acts to boost these doctors into a higher-paying reimbursement bracket.

While the field is short of applicants, with the current emphasis on primary care physicians as well as the proposed Resource-Based Relative Value Scale, internal medicine is one of the primary care specialties that should see higher pay scales, which in turn would make the specialty more attractive to students.

At present there are three hundred eighty-eight training programs for internists, all of which involve three-year residencies. The number of training programs for each of the subspecialties are as follows: cardiovascular disease (cardiology), one hundred seventy-three; clinical cardiac electrophysiology, seventy-nine; critical care medicine, thirty-one; endocrinology, diabetes, and metabolism, one hundred eighteen; gastroenterology, one hundred fifty-five; hematology, fifteen; hematology and oncology, one hundred twenty-one; infectious diseases, one hundred thirty-nine; interventional cardiology, one hundred fifteen; nephrology, one hundred twenty-eight; oncology, twenty-one; pulmonary disease, thirty; pulmonary disease and critical care medicine, one hundred twenty-two; rheumatology, one hundred five; sports medicine, two.

MEDICAL GENETICS

Specialists in this area of medicine deal primarily in the diagnosis and treatment of patients with genetically linked diseases. These include disorders of the metabolism (problems absorbing and digesting food), hemoglobin, chromosome abnormalities, and neural tube defects.

In this area physicians are qualified to identify various genetic diseases through the use of cytogenic, radiologic, and biochemical testing. Using data thus obtained, the medical geneticist can counsel, initiate treatment, or work out plans for the prevention of genetic disease.

Training involves two years in a clinically involved program in pediatrics, ob-gyn, or internal medicine plus two years in clinical genetics with a focus on one of the following subspecialies:

- **Clinical biochemical genetics.** Specialists qualified to perform and interpret biochemical tests to help diagnose and manage genetic disorders.
- **Clinical biochemical/molecular geneticists.** Specialists certified in both clinical biochemical and clinical molecular genetics.
- **Clinical cytogeneticists.** Those in this specialty provide cytogenic laboratory services to diagnose and treat genetic problems.
- **Clinical geneticists.** Specialists in this area can provide comprehensive services in diagnosing, managing, and counseling patients with genetic disorders.

- **Clinical molecular geneticists.** Specialists are qualified to interpret molecular tests involved in treatment of patient genetic problems.
- **Medical geneticists.** These practitioners are consultants to medical and dental specialists in the diagnosis and management of genetic disorders.

Altogether there are forty-seven training programs in medical genetics and eleven in molecular genetic pathology.

NEUROLOGICAL SURGERY

Surgeons in this specialty are among the most highly skilled in all of medicine since it involves all aspects of brain surgery, which due to the delicate nature of the work can have a profound impact on the outcome of the patient's disorder. The outcome can be good, or it can result in disability or death. Because the brain gives us our ability to think, remember, move our limbs, and so forth, the stakes are high. Besides manual dexterity, the neurosurgeon needs to be able to remain cool in the face of pressure or what may appear to be a problematic outcome. New developments in the field of fetal tissue and in the use of microsurgery offer promise for specialists skilled in this specialty.

Conditions seen and treated include brain and spinal cord cancers, lumbar and cervical disk disorders, aneurysms, and head and spinal cord trauma. Besides being able to work effectively under pressure, the neurosurgeon must understand the relationship of the anatomy and physiology to medical health, especially the impact on the nervous system.

Because of the special skills called for, neurosurgeons' salaries are among the most lucrative of all medical specialties, averaging $541,000 in 2004. But it is also one of the most high-risk areas of medicine, vulnerable to malpractice suits, and premiums for insurance coverage are among the highest for all medical specialties.

NEUROLOGY/CHILD NEUROLOGY

Often consultants to other physicians in the diagnosis and treatment of neurological disorders, the neurologist is a highly skilled physician who treats such disorders of the brain and the nervous system as stroke, tumors, muscular dystrophy, meningitis, epilepsy, and Parkinson's disease, among others. Besides their focus on brain disorders, these specialists are concerned with the management of disorders that can impair the function of the spinal cord, peripheral nerves, muscles, and nervous system, as well as the blood vessels involved in these areas.

Because of the close ties between neurology and psychiatry, board certification is offered by the combined board of psychiatry and neurology.

Certification involves four years of postgraduate training, three in neurology after completing one in internal medicine. The subspecialty of child neurology requires additional training. Training is offered in one hundred nineteen programs in neurology and in several subspecialties as follows: child neurology, seventy; clinical neurophysiology, eighty-nine; and pain medicine, one.

NUCLEAR MEDICINE

These specialists use the properties of radioactive atoms and molecules in the diagnosis and detection of disease. A relatively new field, established in 1971, nuclear medicine physicians assist primary care and other physicians in detecting and treating various disorders. Through nuclear medicine, a wide variety of diseases can be uncovered, usually before the organ involved by the disease can be seen to be abnormal through use of other techniques. Examples would be the early detection of coronary artery (heart) disease and early detection and evaluation of cancer, as well as review of the effect of tumor treatment.

Patient contact is limited to the time when patients are involved in various nuclear testing procedures, such as PET (positron-emission tomography); SPECT (single proton emission computerized tomography); MRI (magnetic resonance imaging), and other highly technical procedures of imaging used primarily for diagnostic studies. Nuclear medicine assists and supplements radiology.

Before qualifying for a two-year residency in nuclear medicine, applicants must complete a one- or two-year residency in internal medicine or some other primary care field. There are several combined programs including nuclear medicine and radiology (six years); nuclear medicine and internal medicine (four years); nuclear medicine and cardiology (requires completion of a residency in cardiology plus one additional year in nuclear medicine); and nuclear medicine and neurology (five years). There are sixty-four training programs in nuclear medicine.

OBSTETRICS AND GYNECOLOGY

Specialists in this two-part program deal in the first part, obstetrics, with the care and treatment of women before, during, and after giving birth. The second part, gynecology, is involved with the diseases of the female reproductive system. Although some practitioners specialize in one phase or the other, most work in both and are qualified to do so.

This is one field that seems to be very attractive to women, who account for about sixteen thousand of the forty-two thousand practitioners, or 37 percent. Though the field offers great satisfaction in being involved in the birth process, it does have its negative side relating to the high number of malpractice suits.

Perhaps the malpractice problem relates to the many advances in bio-medical research. One of these advances, ultrasound, is a diagnostic technique that helps the doctor to follow the various stages of the fetus as it develops in the mother's womb from the early stages of pregnancy through to full term. Not only can ultrasound establish the baby's true age, but a sample of the amniotic fluid that envelops the infant in the womb can be checked to see if the child carries any genetic predisposition to such diseases as Downs syndrome, Tay-Sachs disease, or sickle-cell anemia.

Some feel that due to profound medical advances such as ultrasound, patients may have exaggerated or unrealistic expectations of their obstetricians; others contend that competition from other specialists, primarily family physicians and nurse-midwives, has made the obstetrics part of the practice less attractive to those concentrating on gynecology.

Other unattractive aspects of the work, especially in obstetrics, are that practitioners are subject to call any time of the day or night, and that means that the obstetrician must expect to have a certain number of sleepless nights.

But most pregnant women are healthy, and it is doubtful if there is anything quite as satisfying in medicine as the birth of a normal and healthy child.

Under the gynecological hat, specialists in ob-gyn, as it is known in medicine, treat a variety of problems affecting the female reproductive system, including pelvic pain, endometriosis, yeast infections, and cancer of the reproductive organs.

Specialists in gynecology must be able to treat patients both medically and surgically as called for, and because of the hands-on nature of the work they must have good manual dexterity.

While the income is the highest of all the primary care specialties, averaging $261,000 per year in 2004, this is counterbalanced somewhat by the negative aspects of the work—such as the long hours, being subject to calls at any time of the day or night, and the cost of malpractice insurance, among the highest of all medical specialties.

Residencies in ob-gyn last four years, and there are several areas of concentration in the field dealing with reproductive endocrinology, which deals primarily in problems of fertility; gynecological oncology, which involves cancer of the reproductive system; and maternal and fetal medicine, which deals primarily with high-risk pregnancies.

In 2004, there were two hundred fifty-four programs in obstetrics-gynecology.

OPHTHALMOLOGY

This is one specialty in which the practitioner is both a diagnostician and a surgeon. Practitioners do very delicate surgical work, while at the same time serving as primary care physicians to patients with sight problems or with eye care. Ophthalmologists rely on a range of complex equipment in their work.

Although ophthalmologists spend a good deal of their time in the office, they handle the surgical demands of their patients for the most part in specially equipped areas of the hospital operating room.

One of the most important of their duties is the prescription of eyeglasses, for which they rely on refraction equipment that assists them in determining the proper strength of lenses. This is then written in the form of a prescription for eyeglasses. In the case of more severe eye disorders, the ophthalmologist relies on medical treatment or surgery. Patients present themselves with a variety of eye disorders such as glaucoma, a disease characterized by pressure in the eyeball; conjunctivitis, an inflammation of the eye membrane more familiarly known as "pinkeye," and other inflammatory eye problems; and last but certainly not least, cataract.

It is this unique combination of medical treatment and surgical care that makes the field so attractive and challenging. Because they deal with such a small and very sensitive area of the body—the eye—specialists in this area must have excellent eye-hand dexterity and technical skill.

Eye specialists see a mix of patients, young and old, many over long periods, and thus can form some very strong and lasting attachments to patients. But the training is long and rigorous, with residencies running four years, including a year of internship in such patient care fields as internal medicine, pediatrics, neurology, surgery, or family practice.

This is a difficult field to enter, and it currently has an estimated surplus of practitioners. Training is available through approximately one hundred twenty programs.

ORTHOPEDIC SURGERY

Diseases of the musculoskeletal system, including the bones, joints, muscles, and connective tissue, are the main focus of orthopedists, known more familiarly in the profession as orthopods. Conditions that they see and treat regularly in their practices are fractures; degenerative diseases of the hip, knees, shoulders, and elbows; knee trauma; hip trauma; and physical deformities in children and adults. They are also concerned with primary and secondary problems and the effects of central or peripheral nervous lesions of the musculoskeletal system. This is another specialty that involves both diagnosis or cognitive skills and surgery, where called for.

Orthopods are often able to quickly relieve pain. Through surgery or a combination of surgery and other medical treatments such as physical therapy or massage, they are able to correct many potentially crippling conditions, especially arthritis. Such happy outcomes make this a particularly attractive field, but the hours can be long, often twelve to fifteen hours a day.

This is one of the more difficult branches of surgery to enter since it involves a year's internship in orthopedics in general followed by four years of residency involving specific aspects of the field.

If you like to work with your hands and have such hobbies as woodworking or carpentry, orthopedic surgery may be a good field for you. And many orthopods are sports-minded as well. Indeed sports medicine is one of several subspecialties of orthopedics, as are a number of other programs including pediatric orthopedics, orthopedic oncology, hand surgery, foot and ankle surgery, orthopedic trauma, surgery of the spine, and adult reconstructive orthopedics, all of which involve training over and above that needed for orthopedic surgery.

Earnings are high, with specialists averaging $342,000 a year, but this is somewhat offset by the extremely high cost of malpractice insurance and the cost of office equipment and overhead. Currently there are one hundred fifty-two training programs in the general field of orthopedics and many programs in various subspecialties as follows: adult reconstructive orthopedics, thirteen; foot and ankle orthopedics, five; hand surgery, fifty-one; musculoskeletal oncology, nine; orthopedic sports medicine, fifty-eight; surgery of the spine, thirteen; orthopedic trauma, six; and pediatric orthopedics, twenty-four.

OTOLARYNGOLOGY

This specialty deals specifically with disorders of the head—ear, nose, and throat—often referred to in the profession as ENT. It covers virtually all ailments in these areas except for those requiring the services of ophthalmologists (for the eyes) and brain surgeons and neurologists who deal with disorders of the brain and the nervous system.

Disorders that you are apt to be called on to treat in this area include hearing loss; tonsillitis; face, jaw, and other head and neck cancers; allergies; sinus problems; and facial plastic and reconstructive surgery.

In the surgical area, ENT specialists rely on various surgical methods, including microsurgery, laser surgery, and other reconstructive surgery. They must have a vast background in how and when to use various kinds of surgery and skills. But the lines of responsibility are sometimes confusing, and ENT specialists may be in competition with plastic surgeons and other specialists in allergy and pulmonary medicine.

This very competitive specialty involves one year's training in general surgery followed by four years in ENT. Additional training is required in the subspecialties, neurotology and pediatric otolaryngology. There are one hundred two training programs in otolaryngology, eleven in neurotology, and five in pediatric otolaryngology.

PATHOLOGY

Basically practitioners in this specialty work to determine, through various tests—blood chemistry, urinalysis, and others, as well as analysis of organ tissue—if a person is relatively healthy or not or if an organ is healthy or diseased. In the latter case, the pathologist may, for example, take a biopsy or part of an organ removed surgically and examine it under a microscope to see if it is cancerous or not.

In forensic pathology, a subspecialty of the profession, the pathologist conducts autopsies to determine the cause and time of death in cases where these are in question.

Then there is the entire field of blood chemistry, in which the pathologist analyzes blood samples or supervises technicians who analyze the samples for white and red cells, corpuscles, platelets, and cholesterol and fatty substances, all very important indicators of a patient's relative illness or health.

Thus, as an investigator, the pathologist serves as sort of a doctor's doctor, helping the physician to understand if tissue is cancerous, for one thing, or if infection is present in a patient, and then helping to work out a diagnosis as to cause and appropriate treatment of these conditions.

If patient contact is your bag, then this may not be a good field for you because association with patients is almost nil. On the other hand, you will be working with physicians, sometimes very closely, and with technicians and other professional personnel on various medical problems.

Hours are fairly normal and life is low-key, with little of the pressure that characterizes most branches of medicine.

Primarily pathologists direct the operations of the hospital's clinical laboratory as well as their own special duties, so this is almost entirely a hospital-based specialty. Although pathologists' earnings have been high in the past, and still averaged $321,000 in 2004, the enactment of the Resource-Based Relative Value Scale may see pathologists' earnings drop in the future.

Technological advancement in the field has seen the establishment of a number of subspecialties, including the previously mentioned forensic pathology.

For one, there is blood banking, in which the specialist is responsible for maintaining an adequate blood supply for the hospital and for making certain that the blood is used properly.

Other subspecialties include:

- **Cytopathology.** Study of body organs and cells to diagnose various disorders. Cells are studied using special stains and chemical analysis.
- **Dermatopathology.** Specialists diagnose and analyze diseases of the skin.
- **Hematology.** Focuses on diseases that affect the bone marrow, lymph nodes, and above all the blood cells and the blood clotting systems.
- **Immunopathology.** Applying immunological principles to the analysis of cells, tissue, and body fluids for the purpose, among others, of determining the prognosis or outlook of a given disease.
- **Medical microbiology.** The pathologist's expertise is used to identify and isolate microbes that can cause infectious disease.
- **Neuropathology.** Analysis and diagnosis of diseases of the nervous and muscular systems.
- **Pediatric pathology.** Using skills in the diagnosis of diseases affecting fetuses, infants, and children as they develop.

Jobs for pathologists are estimated to be reaching the saturation point, although there always will be some available positions due to pathologists reaching retirement age.

Most of the one hundred fifty-three training programs currently available in pathology involve five years of clinical or anatomic pathology, following completion of a one-year residency in clinical medicine.

The numbers of subspecialty training programs are as follows: blood banking, forty-nine; chemical pathology, four; cytopathology, eighty-six; forensic pathology, forty; hematology, seventy-six; medical microbiology, twelve; neuropathology, thirty-nine; and pediatric pathology, twenty-eight.

PEDIATRICS

Like internal medicine or any of the other primary care fields of medicine, pediatrics focuses on the wide array of diseases—emotional, physical, and social—but their practice is limited to children, from birth to adolescence.

Because of the broad nature of the practice, the pediatrician must have not only a broad background in medicine to treat the array of ailments presented, but special knowledge, understanding, patience, and affection for his or her young charges to be able to withstand the pressure of dealing with anxious parents and ailing youngsters.

Today, due to the vast number of advances of recent years, the emphasis is on wellness or prevention of disease. Indeed most pediatricians stress care of well babies and preventive medicine in the form of proper diet, rest, and inoculation, among others.

Conditions that are commonly seen include developmental and behavioral problems, infectious diseases such as mumps, measles, and whooping cough—which most children are given immunizations for—respiratory and throat diseases, and congenital deformities.

Since children are prone to becoming ill at any time of the day or night, pediatricians often work long days and are subject to many interruptions when away from the office. The hours are long, averaging a 58.6-hour workweek, with about 65 percent of that time spent in the office, 19 percent in the hospital, and 16 percent in surgical and other procedures.

As a primary care physician working mainly in cognitive or diagnostic procedures to treat the ailments presented, the pediatrician is in the lower bracket when it comes to salary, averaging about $175,000 in 2004 before taxes. Women currently comprise more than half of the total number of pediatricians, with thirty-eight thousand working in this specialty.

There are two hundred two training programs in pediatrics involving a three-year residency, after which pediatricians can pursue fellowships in various subspecialties with more training as listed here:

- **Adolescent medicine.** Specialists trained in the unique physical, psychological, and social characteristics of children and adolescents, their health problems and their needs.
- **Neonatal-perinatal pediatrics.** The branch of pediatrics dealing with the care of high-risk infants.
- **Pediatric cardiology.** The specialty that covers cardiovascular care of children, from fetus to young adult.
- **Pediatric critical care.** The pediatrician focusing on advanced life support for children from birth or just before birth to adolescence.
- **Pediatric emergency medicine.** A pediatrician qualified to manage emergencies in infants and children.
- **Pediatric endocrinology.** Specialist in providing care to infants, children, and adolescents with diseases resulting from an

abnormality in the endocrine glands—such as diabetes, growth problems, birth defects, and disorders of the genitals, the thyroid, or the adrenal and pituitary glands.

- **Pediatric gastroenterology.** The focus of this children's specialist is on disorders of the digestive system of infants, children, and adolescents.
- **Medical toxicology.** This children's specialist focuses on patients suffering from poisoning resulting from exposure to prescription and nonprescription medications, illegal drugs, household or industrial toxins, and other poisonous substances.
- **Neurodevelopmental disabilities.** This specialist consults, educates, and assumes leadership in the management and early identification of children with neurodevelopmental disorders.
- **Pediatric hematology-oncology.** A pediatric specialist trained to recognize and manage pediatric blood disorders and cancerous conditions.
- **Pediatric infectious diseases.** This pediatrician is trained to care for children in the diagnosis, treatment, and prevention of infectious diseases.
- **Pediatric nephrology.** This specialist deals primarily with diseases of the kidneys and urinary tract in children.
- **Pediatric pulmonology.** Pediatrician dedicated to the diagnosis, care, and treatment of respiratory diseases affecting children and infants.
- **Pediatric rheumatology.** This children's specialist is concerned with the prevention, identification, and treatment of rheumatic and related diseases affecting the muscles and joints, including juvenile rheumatoid arthritis.
- **Sports medicine.** The focus of this pediatrician is the care of children with medical problems involving exercise and recreational competitive sports.

Besides the training programs specifically for pediatricians, the number of training programs offered in various pediatric subspecialties is as follows: adolescent medicine, twenty-five; neonatal and perinatal medicine, ninety-six; pediatric cardiology, forty-eight; pediatric critical care medicine, fifty-eight; pediatric emergency medicine, forty-three; pediatric endocrinology, sixty-two; pediatric gastroenterology, fifty-one; pediatric hematology/oncology, sixty; pediatric infectious diseases, sixty; pediatric nephrology, forty; pediatric pulmonology, forty-six; pediatric rheumatology, twenty-three; and pediatric sports medicine, eight.

PHYSICAL MEDICINE AND REHABILITATION

A physician certified in physical medicine and rehabilitation is often called a physiatrist. The physiatrist's primary function is the diagnosis and treatment of patients with muscular, neurologic, cardiovascular, and other body impairments. The primary goal of this specialist is to achieve maximum restoration of physical, psychological, social, and vocational function through a comprehensive program of rehabilitation. Pain management is often an important part of the physiatrist's role.

A relatively new field, the practice, primarily hospital based, involves helping to restore stroke or accident patients to health or helping patients suffering from various neurological ailments, such as multiple sclerosis and Guillain-Barre syndrome, to maximize their ability to function.

The specialty calls for a broad background in orthopedics, neurology, psychiatry, urology, and geriatrics. Contact with patients is frequent, and hours are fairly regular. Training, offered in seventy-nine programs, involves three years in physical medicine following completion of a one-year residency in internal medicine.

Training programs involving additional study are also offered in two subspecialty programs: pain management (seven programs) and spinal cord injury medicine (twenty programs). The outlook for specialists in this field looks promising for the foreseeable future.

PLASTIC SURGERY

Many might consider this the most glamorous of the medical specialties with many of these specialists involved in helping show business, sports, and other celebrities to get rid of unwarranted wrinkles and blemishes and in making their noses and facial features more attractive. But most of these specialists are involved in more routine activities, such as helping victims of burns and accidents and patients with birth defects to be restored to a more attractive appearance and to restore the normal function of their limbs.

Besides nose restoration, plastic surgeons treat many patients with such congenital deformities as scars, lesions, birthmarks, and other disfigurements as well as facial trauma, cancer, and degenerative diseases. In their work they often use many new surgical procedures, such as liposuction for thighs and microsurgery. In addition, plastic surgeons must possess special knowledge and skill in surgery of grafts, flaps, and free tissue transfer. A sense of the artistic is called for. Much of the work is performed on an outpatient basis, and night work is often involved in this field.

Since practitioners are often able to accomplish a marked improvement in the patient's appearance, the work offers these specialists a good deal of satisfaction. On the other hand, the plastic surgeon is prone to encountering one of the major hazards of the practice—the patients' often unrealistic expectations of what the surgeon can do to make them look better. As a result, the field is one of those areas in medicine most prone to malpractice suits and resultant prohibitive expenses in obtaining insurance coverage. At the same time, earnings of these specialists are among the highest of all in medicine, with individual doctors averaging $412,000 a year.

This is a highly competitive field with a surplus of specialists foreseen for the near future. It takes three years of general surgery followed by two to three years of training in plastic surgery to qualify for certification. There are currently eighty-eight training programs in the field as well as training programs that require additional study in the following subspecialties: craniofacial surgery (five programs) and hand surgery (thirteen programs).

PREVENTIVE MEDICINE

This branch of medicine focuses on the health of individuals and defined populations in order to promote and maintain good health through prevention of disease, disability, and premature death. These specialists work to eliminate unnecessary public hazards such as environmental dangers and illness due to smoking and alcoholism.

There are three primary routes to certification: aerospace medicine, occupational or industrial medicine, and public health medicine. A broad background in epidemiology, health education and policy, nutrition, and health services administration and management is required for certification in preventive medicine.

Most specialists in this field hold positions in public health agencies at the local, state, or federal levels or are attached to the armed forces or to private industry.

The work is composed of several distinct areas of concentration: application of biostatistical principles and methods; application of epidemiology to population; health services administration; evaluating population health and disease management programs; and control of environmental forces that can adversely affect health. In addition to completing all of the courses required for certification, applicants in this field must have a master of public health degree or the equivalent. Training lasts three years and is offered in eighty-four programs.

Certification in one of the following subspecialties involves additional training:

- **Medical toxicology.** A specialist in the treatment and management of patients suffering accidental or intentional poisoning through exposure to prescription and nonprescription medications, drug abuse, household or industrial toxins, and poisonous elements in the environment.
- **Undersea and hyperbaric medicine.** According to the American Board of Medical Specialties, undersea and hyperbaric medical specialists treat decompression illness and diving accidents and use hyperbaric oxygen therapy to treat such conditions as carbon monoxide poisoning, gas gangrene, nonhealing wounds, and tissue damage from radiation and burns.

At present there are three training programs in medical toxicology and one in undersea and hyperbaric medicine.

PSYCHIATRY

Psychiatrists treat and diagnose disorders of the mind, including schizophrenia and other psychotic disorders, mood and anxiety disorders, and sexual and identity disorders, among others. In the past psychiatrists have used various types of therapy to treat patients, including hydrotherapy (immersion in water tanks), psychotherapy (used primarily by followers of Sigmund Freud), and shock treatment.

Today, however, more emphasis is being placed on psychotropic medications, which are very effective and provide the psychiatrist with an arsenal of drugs that he or she can use in controlling mental disease. Working primarily out of their own offices, psychiatrists also are attached to community health centers, psychiatric and short-term hospitals (which treat primarily short-term acute disorders), and substance abuse centers.

Perhaps more than any other medical specialty, psychiatry is people oriented and practitioners must be able to see things from the patient's perspective—get into the patient's mind, so to speak. While many conditions are chronic and debilitating over the years, psychiatrists nevertheless can help a good deal, through their understanding and support, to make life a little better and more fulfilling for both patients and their families. Quite often they can help patients with mental problems stemming from physical disorders (psychosomatic medicine) and short-term illnesses such as alcoholism or drug abuse, to regain their emotional balance and continue to function as normal human beings.

While hours are for the most part fairly regular, salaries, whether you are in solo practice or attached to a private clinic, tend to be on the low side, averaging $169,000 in 2004. Training consists of a year's internship followed by three years in psychiatry with a heavy neurological component, because many psychiatric disorders are rooted in neurological problems that affect the brain.

With additional training, psychiatrists can be certified in several subspecialties:

- **Addiction psychiatry.** This subspecialty deals with addictive disorders and emotional problems related to addiction and substance abuse.
- **Child and adolescent psychiatry.** This subspecialty focuses on mental, addictive, and emotional disorders of children.
- **Clinical neurophysiology.** Central and peripheral nervous system disorders are the concern of this specialist, who uses a variety of electrophysiological procedures.
- **Forensic psychiatry.** This specialist evaluates individuals involved with the legal system and provides specialized treatment to those held in jails, prisons, and forensic psychiatry hospitals.

• **Geriatric psychiatry.** This specialist understands the special needs of the elderly in diagnosing and managing the treatment of their mental disorders and emotional problems.

At present one hundred eighty-two training programs are being offered in psychiatry, and a number are offered in the subspecialties as follows: addiction psychiatry, forty-seven; child and adolescent psychiatry, one hundred fifteen; forensic psychiatry, forty-two; geriatric psychiatry, sixty; and clinical neurophysiology, eighty-nine.

RADIOLOGY

Specialists in this branch of medicine work primarily in two areas of radiology—diagnostic, which accounts for one of the more than fourteen thousand practitioners in this specialty, and radiation oncology, in which specialists use sophisticated equipment in treating malignancies and other diseases.

In the diagnostic area of the field, specialists use complex x-ray and other imaging equipment to supply the data and photos physicians need to arrive at a diagnosis of a given problem.

Equipment and procedures, which are highly technical and constantly evolving, include MRI (magnetic resonance imaging), CT (computerized tomography) scanners, PET (positron-emission tomography), as well as radioactive isotopes (nuclear medicine) and ultrasound. This specialist is primarily a consultant to physicians in interpreting x-ray film and the results of the various tests. The range of problems seen is as broad as medicine itself and includes fractures, gastric disorders, cardiovascular problems, pulmonary diseases, and many others.

Radiation oncology is a rapidly evolving and comparatively new field involving complex equipment such as cobalt treatment centers and radiographic treatment of malignancies.

As new technology evolves, the field is constantly expanding, and these specialists must spend a good deal of time keeping abreast of new developments.

Operating primarily behind the scenes, these specialists rarely, if ever, develop long-term relationships with patients. However they do work closely with referring physicians and their own technical staffs and nurses.

In 2004 there were two hundred seventy training programs in the entire field, involving four years of residency. With additional training, radiologists can be certified in several subspecialties as follows:

- **Radiological physics.** These specialists deal with the diagnostic and therapeutic applications of x-rays, gamma rays from sealed sources, and ultrasonic radiation, as well as the equipment associated with radiation safety.
- **Neuroradiology.** A subspecialty utilizing imaging procedures as they relate to the brain, spine and spinal cord, head, neck, and organs of special sense in patients.
- **Nuclear radiology.** Here specialists are involved in the analysis and imaging of radionuclides and radiolabeled substances and the administration of radionuclides for the treatment of disease.
- **Pediatric radiology.** Radiologists with skills in the imaging of disorders of newborns, infants, and children.
- **Vascular and interventional radiology.** Specialists who diagnose and treat diseases by various invasive techniques based on radiologic imaging including fluoroscopy, digital radiography, computerized tomography, sonography, and MRI.

In 2004 training programs were offered in these various radiology subspecialties as follows: abdominal radiology, eight; digestive radiology, one hundred ninety-three, cardiothoracic radiology, two; endovascular surgical neuroradiology, eight; neuroradiology, eighty-seven, musculoskeletal radiology, eight; nuclear radiology, nineteen; pediatric radiology, forty; and vascular and interventional radiology, one hundred four.

GENERAL SURGERY

A surgeon manages the wide variety of surgical conditions affecting almost every area of the body. These specialists use a variety of diagnostic techniques, including endoscopy, for observing internal organs, and may use special instruments during surgical operations. They are expected to know the main features of other surgical specialties so that they can recognize problems in those areas and know when to refer a patient to another specialist.

Training involving five years of residency is available in two hundred fifty-three programs. Additional training qualifies surgeons for certification in several subspecialties as follows:

- **Pediatric surgery.** A surgeon with expertise in the management of surgical conditions of premature and newborn infants, children, and adolescents.
- **Surgery of the hand.** A specialist with skills in the management of disorders of the hand and wrist.
- **Surgical critical care.** These specialists are skilled in the management of critically ill and postoperative patients, and in the diagnosis and treatment of patients with multiple organ dysfunction. They may be in charge of hospital intensive care units and work with and support patient care among the primary care physicians, the critical care staff, and other specialists.

Certification of these surgical subspecialties involves additional training and programs are available as follows: hand surgery, three programs; pediatric surgery, thirty programs; vascular surgery, ninety-three programs.

THORACIC SURGERY

This branch of surgery deals with medical problems of the chest cavity—including the heart, arteries leading to the heart, aneurysms, and lungs. Perhaps more than any other branch of medicine, except for brain surgery, these specialists need to be able to work under pressure and to work swiftly with manual dexterity and stamina. Due to the nature of the work, thoracic surgeons frequently see dramatic and swift changes for the better in their patients' health, thus the work can be very satisfying.

While salaries of these specialists are among the highest in all medicine, averaging $515,000 in 2004, the expenses, particularly for malpractice coverage, are also high.

Symptomatic of the vast amount of knowledge and skills required for this work is the training period—the lengthiest in medicine—involving a five-year internship and residency in general surgery, followed by a three-year fellowship in thoracic surgery. The field is very competitive, and a considerable excess of practitioners is seen for the near future.

Ninety-two training programs in this specialty were offered in 2004.

UROLOGY

Another specialty that is both surgical and medical in approach is urology, which focuses on diseases of the genitourinary tract, including the kidneys, bladder, and urethra, and, in males, the prostate and the genitals.

Relying considerably on diagnostic techniques, urologists often use medical treatments—drugs primarily—to effect cures for their patients. Conditions encountered range from mild and easily treated to acute and very uncomfortable.

Since conditions treated often are long range, urologists often develop personal and satisfying relationships with their patients. The field is one in which technology is used to great effect in working out cures and positive results, such as shock wave lithotripsy (effective in dissolving kidney and gallstones), prostate ultrasound, and endoscopic surgery. Besides a deep understanding of physiology and anatomy, urologists need exceptional manual dexterity and coordination.

The pay in this field averaged $358,000 in 2004, but training is lengthy. The one hundred twenty-one training programs available in 2004 require a two-year residency and internship followed by three years in urology. Predictions for the estimated need of urologists call for a considerable surplus in the immediate future.

APPENDIX A

MEDICAL SCHOOLS OF THE UNITED STATES AND CANADA

UNITED STATES SCHOOLS

Alabama

University of Alabama School of
Medicine
University of Alabama at
Birmingham
1813 Sixth Avenue S.
Birmingham, AL 35294-3293

University of South Alabama
College of Medicine
307 University Boulevard
Mobile, AL 36688
southalabama.edu

Arizona

University of Arizona College of
Medicine
Arizona Health Sciences Center
1501 N. Campbell Avenue
P.O. Box 245018
Tucson, AZ 85724-5018
medicine.arizona.edu

Arkansas

University of Arkansas for Medical
Sciences
College of Medicine
4301 W. Markham Street
Little Rock, AR 72205
uams.edu/com

California

Keck School of Medicine of the
University of Southern
California
1975 Zonal Avenue, KAM 500
Los Angeles, CA 90033
usc.edu/schools/medicine/ksom
.html

Loma Linda University School of
Medicine
Loma Linda, CA 92350
llu.edu/llu/medicine

Stanford University School of
Medicine
300 Pasteur Drive
Always Building M121
Stanford, CA 94305-5119
med.stanford.edu

University of California, Davis
School of Medicine
One Shields Avenue
Davis, CA 95616-8640
som.ucdavis.edu

University of California, Irvine
College of Medicine
Irvine, CA 92697-3950
ucihs.uci.edu/com

David Geffen School of Medicine,
UCLA
10833 Le Conte Avenue
Los Angeles, CA 90095
dgsom.healthsciences.ucla.edu

University of California, San Diego
School of Medicine
La Jolla, CA 92093
medicine.ucsd.edu

University of California, San
Francisco
School of Medicine
513 Parnassus Avenue
San Francisco, CA 94143-0410
medschool.ucsf.edu

Colorado

University of Colorado Health
Sciences Center
School of Medicine
4200 E. Ninth Avenue
Denver, CO 80262
uchsc.edu/sm/sm/offdean.htm

Connecticut

University of Connecticut School
of Medicine
263 Farmington Avenue
Farmington, CT 06030
medicine.uchc.edu

Yale University School of Medicine
333 Cedar Street
P.O. Box 208055
New Haven, CT 06520-8055
info.med.yale.edu/ysm

District of Columbia

George Washington University
School of Medicine and Health
Sciences
2300 Eye Street NW
Washington, DC 20037
gwumc.edu/smhs

Georgetown University School of
Medicine
3900 Reservoir Road NW
Washington, DC 20007
som.georgetown.edu

Howard University College of
Medicine
520 W Street NW
Washington, DC 20059
med.howard.edu

Florida

Florida State University College of
Medicine
1269 W. Call Street
Tallahassee, FL 32306-4300
med.fsu.edu

University of Florida College of
Medicine
Box 100215
J. Hillis Miller Health Center
Gainesville, FL 32610
med.ufl.edu

University of Miami School of
Medicine
1600 NW Tenth Avenue
P.O. Box 016099(R699)
Miami, FL 33101
med.miami.edu

University of South Florida College
of Medicine
12901 Bruce B. Downs Boulevard
Box 2
Tampa, FL 33612-4799
med.usf.edu/medicine

Georgia

Emory University School of
Medicine
Woodruff Health Sciences Building
Administration Building
1440 Clifton Road NE
Atlanta, GA 30322
med.emory.edu./index.cfm

Medical College of Georgia
School of Medicine
1120 Fifteenth Street
Augusta, GA 30912
mcg.edu/som/index.html

Mercer University School of
Medicine
1550 College Street
Macon, GA 31207
medicine.mercer.edu

Morehouse School of Medicine
720 Westview Drive SW
Atlanta, GA 30310
msm.edu

Hawaii

University of Hawaii
John A. Burns School of Medicine
1960 East-West Road
Honolulu, HI 96822
hawaiimed.hawaii.edu

Illinois

Rosalind Franklin University of
    Medicine and Science
The Chicago Medical School
3333 Green Bay Road
North Chicago, IL 60064
rosalindfranklin.edu./cms

Loyola University Chicago Stritch
    School of Medicine
2150 S. First Avenue
Maywood, IL 60153
meddean.luc.edu/default.cfm

Northwestern University
Feinberg School of Medicine
303 E. Chicago Avenue
Chicago, IL 60611-3008
medschool.northwestern.edu

Rush Medical College of Rush
    University
600 S. Paulina Street
Chicago, IL 60612
rushu.rush.edu/medcol

Southern Illinois University School
    of Medicine
801 N. Rutledge
P.O. Box 19620
Springfield, IL 62794-9620
siumed.edu

University of Chicago
Division of Biological Sciences
The Pritzker School of Medicine
5841 S. Maryland Avenue, MC1000
Chicago, IL 60637-1470
pritzker.bsd.uchicago.edu

University of Illinois College of
    Medicine
1853 W. Polk Street, MC 784
Chicago, IL 60612
uic.edu/depts/mcam

Indiana

Indiana University School of
    Medicine
Indiana University Medical Center
1120 South Drive
Indianapolis, IN 46202-5114
medicine.iu.edu

Iowa

University of Iowa
Roy J. and Lucille A. Carver College
    of Medicine
200 Medicine Administration
    Building
Iowa City, IA 52242-1101
medicine.uiowa.edu

Kansas

University of Kansas School of
    Medicine
3901 Rainbow Boulevard
Kansas City, KS 66160-7300
kumc.edu/som/som.html

Kentucky

University of Kentucky College of
　Medicine
MN-150
Chandler Medical Center
Lexington, KY 40536-0298
mc.uky.edu/medicine

University of Louisville School of
　Medicine
Abell Administration Center
323 E. Chestnut Street
Louisville, IL 40202-3866
louisville.edu/medschool

Louisiana

Louisiana State University
School of Medicine in New Orleans
533 Bolivar Street
New Orleans, LA 70112-2822
medschool.lsuhsc.edu

Louisiana State University
School of Medicine in Shreveport
P.O. Box 33932
Shreveport, LA 71130-3932
sh.lsuhsc.edu/medschool/index
　.html

Tulane University School of
　Medicine
1430 Tulane Avenue
New Orleans, LA 70112
som.tulane.edu

Maryland

Johns Hopkins University School
　of Medicine
720 Rutland Avenue
Baltimore, MD 21205
hopkinsmedicine.org/som/index
　.html

Uniformed Services University of
　the Health Sciences
F. Edward Hebert School of
　Medicine
4301 Jones Bridge Road
Bethesda, MD 20814-4799
usuhs.mil

University of Maryland School of
　Medicine
655 W. Baltimore Street
Baltimore, MD 21201
medschool.umaryland.edu

Massachusetts

Boston University School of
　Medicine
715 Albany Street
Boston, MA 02118
bumc.bu.edu/busm

Harvard Medical School
25 Shattuck Street
Boston, MA 02115
hms.harvard.edu/hms/home.asp

Tufts University School of
Medicine
136 Harrison Avenue
Boston, MA 02111
tufts.edu/med

University of Massachusetts
Medical School
55 Lake Avenue N.
Worcester, MA 01655-0112
umassmed.edu

Michigan

Michigan State University
College of Human Medicine
A-110 East Fee Hall
East Lansing, MI 48824
humanmedicine.msu.edu

University of Michigan Medical
School
1301 Catherine Road
Medical Science Building I
Ann Arbor, MI 48109-0624
med.umich.edu/medschool

Wayne State University
School of Medicine
540 East Canfield Avenue
Detroit, MI 48201
med.wayne.edu

Minnesota

Mayo Medical School
200 First Street SW
Rochester, MN 55905
medicalschooladmission.com/mayo

University of Minnesota Medical
School—Twin Cities
Mayo Mail Code 293
420 Delaware Street SE
Minneapolis, MN 55455
med.umn.edu

Mississippi

University of Mississippi School of
Medicine
2500 N. State Street
Jackson, MS 39216
som.umc.edu

Missouri

Saint Louis University
School of Medicine
1402 S. Grand Boulevard
St. Louis, MO 63104
slu.edu/colleges/med

University of Missouri—Columbia
School of Medicine
MA202 Medical Sciences Building
One Hospital Drive
Columbia, MO 65212
hsc.missouri.edu/~medicine

University of Missouri—
Kansas City
School of Medicine
2411 Holmes Street
Kansas City, MO 64108-2792
research.med.umkc.edu

Washington University in St. Louis
School of Medicine
660 S. Euclid Avenue
Box 8106
St. Louis, MO 63110
medicine.wustl.edu

Nebraska
Creighton University
School of Medicine
2500 California Plaza
Omaha, NE 68178
medicine.creighton.edu

University of Nebraska
College of Medicine
986545 Nebraska Medical Center
Omaha, NE 68198-6545
app1.unmc.edu/uncom/index.cfm

Nevada
University of Nevada
School of Medicine
Savitt Medical Building/332
Reno, NV 89557-0046
unr.edu/med

New Hampshire
Dartmouth Medical School
1 Rope Ferry Road
Hanover, NH 03755-1404
dms.dartmouth.edu

New Jersey
UMDNJ–New Jersey Medical
    School
185 S. Orange Avenue
Newark, NJ 07103-2714
njms.umdnj.edu

UMDNJ–Robert Wood Johnson
    Medical School
675 Hoes Lane
Piscataway, NJ 08854-5635
rwjms.umdnj.edu

New Mexico
University of New Mexico
School of Medicine
Albuquerque, NM 87131
hsc.unm.edu/som

New York
Albany Medical College
Mail Code 34, Room MS-129
47 New Scotland Avenue
Albany, NY 12208
amc.edu

Albert Einstein College of Medicine
    of Yeshiva University
1300 Morris Park Avenue
Bronx, NY 10461
aecom.yu.edu/home

Columbia University College of
    Physicians and Surgeons
630 W. 168th Street
New York, NY 10032
cpmcnet.columbia.edu/dept/ps

Joan and Sanford I. Weill Medical
    College of Cornell University
1300 York Avenue
New York, NY 10021
med.cornell.edu

Mount Sinai School of Medicine of
New York University
One Gustave L. Levy Place
New York, NY 10029-6574
mssm.edu

New York Medical College
Administration Building
Valhalla, NY 10595
nymc.edu

New York University School of
Medicine
550 First Avenue
New York, NY 10016
med.nyu.edu

State University of New York
Downstate Medical Center
College of Medicine
450 Clarkson Avenue, Box 97
Brooklyn, NY 11203-2098
hscbklyn.edu

State University of New York
Upstate Medical University
750 E. Adams Street
Syracuse, NY 13210
upstate.edu

Stony Brook University Health
Sciences Center
School of Medicine
Level 4, Room 169
Stony Brook, NY 11794-8430
hsc.stonybrook.edu/som

University at Buffalo, The State
University of New York
School of Medicine and Biomedical
Sciences
3435 Main Street
Buffalo, NY 14214
smbs.buffalo.edu

University of Rochester School of
Medicine and Dentistry
601 Elmwood Avenue
Rochester, NY 14642
urmc.rochester.edu/smd

North Carolina

The Brody School of Medicine at
East Carolina University
Greenville, NC 27858-4354
ecu.edu/med

Duke University School of
Medicine
P.O. Box 3701
Durham, NC 27710
medschool.duke.edu

University of North Carolina at
Chapel Hill
School of Medicine
Chapel Hill, NC 27599
med.unc.edu

Wake Forest University School of
Medicine
Medical Center Boulevard
Winston-Salem, NC 27157
wfubmc.edu

North Dakota

University of North Dakota School
   of Medicine and Health Sciences
501 N. Columbia Road
Box 9037
Grand Forks, ND 58202-9037
med.und.nodak.edu

Ohio

Case Western Reserve University
School of Medicine
10900 Euclid Avenue
Cleveland, OH 44106-4915
mediswww.meds.cwru.edu

Medical University of Ohio at
   Toledo
P.O. Box 10008
Toledo, OH 43699-0008
meduohio.edu/smed/smedmain
   .html

Northeastern Ohio Universities
   College of Medicine
4209 State Route 44
P.O. Box 95
Rootstown, OH 44272-0095
neoucom.edu

Ohio State University College of
   Medicine and Public Health
254 Meiling Hall
370 W. Ninth Avenue
Columbus, OH 43210-1238
medicine.osu.edu

University of Cincinnati College
   of Medicine
P.O. Box 670555
Cincinnati, OH 45267-0555
med.uc.edu

Wright State University School
   of Medicine
P.O. Box 927
Dayton, OH 45401-0927
med.wright.edu

Oklahoma

University of Oklahoma College
   of Medicine
P.O. Box 26901
Oklahoma City, OK 73190
medicine.ouhsc.edu

Oregon

Oregon Health and Science
   University
School of Medicine
3181 SW Sam Jackson Park Road
Portland, OR 97201-3098
ohsu.edu/som

Pennsylvania

Drexel University College of
   Medicine
2900 Queen Lane
Philadelphia, PA 19129
drexel.edu/med

Jefferson Medical College of
  Thomas Jefferson University
1025 Walnut Street
Philadelphia, PA 19107-5083
jefferson.edu/jmc

Pennsylvania State University
College of Medicine
500 University Drive
P.O. Box 850
Hershey, PA 17033
hmc.psu.edu/college

Temple University School of
  Medicine
3400 N. Broad Street
Philadelphia, PA 19140
medschool.temple.edu

University of Pennsylvania Health
  System
3620 Hamilton Walk
Philadelphia, PA 19104-6055
uphs.upenn.edu

University of Pittsburgh School
  of Medicine
M240 Scaife Hall
3550 Terrace Street
Pittsburgh, PA 15261
medschool.pitt.edu

Puerto Rico
Ponce School of Medicine
P.O. Box 7004
Ponce, PR 00732
psm.edu

Universidad Central del Caribe
School of Medicine
Call Box 60-327
Bayamon, PR 00960-6032
uccaribe.edu

University of Puerto Rico
School of Medicine
Medical Sciences Campus
P.O. Box 365067
San Juan, PR 00936-5067
rcm.upr.edu

Rhode Island
Brown Medical School
97 Waterman Street
Providence, RI 02912
bms.brown.edu

South Carolina
Medical University of South
  Carolina
College of Medicine
96 Jonathan Lucas Street
Charleston, SC 29425
musc.edu/com/com1.html

University of South Carolina
School of Medicine
Columbia, SC 29208
med.sc.edu

South Dakota
University of South Dakota
School of Medicine
1400 W. Twenty-second
Sioux Falls, SD 57105-1570
usd.edu/med

Tennessee

East Tennessee State University
James H. Quillen College of
   Medicine
P.O. Box 70694
Johnson City, TN 37614
com.etsu.edu

Meharry Medical College School of
   Medicine
1005 D. B. Todd Jr. Boulevard
Nashville, TN 37204
mmc.edu

University of Tennessee Health
   Science Center
College of Medicine
800 Madison Avenue
Memphis TN 38163
utmem.edu/medicine

Vanderbilt University School of
   Medicine
Twenty-first Avenue S. at Garland
   Avenue
Nashville, TN 37232
mc.vanderbilt.edu/medschool

Texas

Baylor College of Medicine
One Baylor Plaza
Houston, TX 77030
bcm.edu

The Texas A & M University
   System Health Science Center
College of Medicine
147 Joe H. Reynolds Medical
   Building
1114 TAMU
College Station, TX 77843-1114
medicine.tamu.edu

Texas Tech University Health
   Sciences Center
School of Medicine
3601 Fourth Street
Lubbock, TX 79430
ttuhsc.edu

University of Texas Medical Branch
   at Galveston
301 University Boulevard
Galveston, TX 77555
som.utmb.edu

University of Texas Medical School
   at San Antonio
7703 Floyd Curl Drive
San Antonio, TX 78229-3900
som.uthscsa.edu

University of Texas Medical School
   at Houston
6431 Fannin Street
Houston, TX 77030
med.uth.tmc.edu

University of Texas Southwestern
  Medical School
5323 Harry Hines Boulevard
Dallas, TX 75390
utsouthwestern.edu/home/
  education/medicalschool/
  index.html

Utah

University of Utah
School of Medicine
30 N. 1900 E.
Salt Lake City, UT 84132-2101
uuhsc.utah.edu/som

Vermont

The University of Vermont
College of Medicine
E109 Given Building
Burlington, VT 05405
med.uvm.edu

Virginia

Eastern Virginia Medical School
P.O. Box 1980
Norfolk, VA 23501
evms.edu

University of Virginia
School of Medicine
P.O. Box 800793-McKim Hall
Charlottesville, VA 22908
healthsystem.virginia.edu/
  education-research/medschl.cfm

Virginia Commonwealth University
School of Medicine
P.O. Box 980565
Richmond, VA 23298-0565
medschool.vcu.edu

Washington

University of Washington
School of Medicine
Seattle, WA 98195-6340
uwmedicine.org/facilities/uwschool
  ofmedicine

West Virginia

Marshall University
Joan C. Edwards School of
  Medicine
1600 Medical Center Drive
Huntington, WV 25701-3655
musom.marshall.edu

West Virginia University
School of Medicine
Morgantown, WV 26506
hsc.wvu.edu/som

Wisconsin

Medical College of Wisconsin
8701 Watertown Plank Road
Milwaukee, WI 53226
mcw.edu

University of Wisconsin Medical
  School
1300 University Avenue
Madison, WI 53706
med.wisc.edu

CANADIAN SCHOOLS

Alberta

University of Alberta
Faculty of Medicine and Dentistry
2J2 Mackenzie Health Sciences
  Centre
Edmonton, AB T6G 2R7
med.ualberta.ca

University of Calgary
Faculty of Medicine
3330 Hospital Drive NW
Calgary, AB T2N 4N1
faculty.med.ucalgary.ca

British Columbia

University of British Columbia
Faculty of Medicine
317-2194 Health Sciences Mall
Vancouver, BC V6T 1Z3
med.ubc.ca

Manitoba

University of Manitoba
Faculty of Medicine
753 McDermot Avenue
Winnipeg, MB R3E OW3
umanitoba.ca/faculties/medicine

Newfoundland

Memorial University of
  Newfoundland
Faculty of Medicine
Health Sciences Centre
Prince Philip Drive
St. John's, NF A1B 3V6
med.mun.ca/med

Nova Scotia

Dalhousie University
Faculty of Medicine
CRC Building, Room C-205
5849 University Avenue
Halifax, NS B3H 4H7
medicine.dal.ca

Ontario

McMaster University
School of Medicine
Health Sciences Centre
Room 1B7
1200 Main Street W.
Hamilton, ON L8N 3Z5
fhs.mcmaster.ca

Queen's University
Faculty of Health Sciences
Kingston, ON K7L 3N6
meds.queensu.ca

University of Ottawa
Faculty of Medicine
451 Smyth Road
Ottawa, ON K1H 8M5
medecine.uottawa.ca

University of Toronto
Faculty of Medicine
1 King's College Circle
Toronto, ON M5S 1A8
facmed.utoronto.ca

University of Western Ontario
Faculty of Medicine and Dentistry
Health Sciences Addition
Richmond Street N.
London, ON N6A 5C1
med.uwo.ca

Quebec

Université Laval
Faculté de médecine
Québec City, QC G1K 7P4
www.fmed.ulaval.ca

McGill University
Faculty of Medicine
3655 Promenade Sir-William-Osler
Montreal, QC H3G 1Y6
med.mcgill.ca

Université de Montréal
Faculté de médecine
CP 6128, Succ. Centre-ville
Montréal, QC H3C 3J7
med.umontreal.ca

Université de Sherbrooke
Faculté de médecine et des Sciences
   de la Santé
3001, 12e Avenue Nord
Sherbrooke, QC JlH 5N4
usherbrooke.ca/medecine

Saskatchewan

University of Saskatchewan
College of Medicine
B103 Health Sciences Building
107 Wiggins Road
Saskatoon, SK S7N 5E5
usask.ca/medicine

APPENDIX B

MEDICAL ORGANIZATIONS AND SPECIALTY BOARDS

MEDICAL ORGANIZATIONS

Accreditation Council for Graduate
   Medical Education
515 N. State Street
Chicago, IL 60610-4322
acgme.org

Aerospace Medical Association
320 S. Henry Street
Alexandria, VA 22314
asma.org

American Academy of Allergy and
   Immunology
85 W. Algonquin Road, Suite 55
Arlington Heights, IL 60005
aaai.org

American Academy of Child and
   Adolescent Psychiatry
3615 Wisconsin Street NW
Washington, DC 20005
aacap.org

American Academy of
   Dermatology
930 E. Woodfield Road
Schaumburg, IL 60173
aad.org

American Academy of Family
   Physicians
114 Tomahawk Creek Parkway
Leawood, KS 66211-2672
familydoctor.org

American Academy of Neurology
1080 Montreal Avenue
St. Paul, MN 55116
aan.org

American Academy of
   Ophthalmology
P.O. Box 7424
San Francisco, CA 94120-7424
aao.org

American Academy of Orthopaedic
   Surgeons
6300 N. River Road
Rosemont, IL 60018-4262
aaos.org

American Academy of
   Otolaryngology
One Prince Street
Alexandria, VA 22314-3157
entnet.org

American Academy of Pediatrics
141 Northwest Point Boulevard
Elk Grove Village, IL 60009-0927
aap.org

American Academy of Physical
   Medicine and Rehabilitation
One IBM Plaza
Chicago, IL 60611-3604
aapmr.org

American Academy of Psychiatry
   and the Law
One Regency Drive, P.O. Box 30
Bloomfield, CT 06002
aapl.org

American Association of Colleges
   of Osteopathic Medicine
5555 Friendship Boulevard,
   Suite 310
Chevy Chase, MD 20815-7231
aacom.org

American Association of
   Neurological Surgeons
5550 Meadowbrook Drive
Rolling Meadows, IL 60008
aans.org

The American Association for
   Thoracic Surgery
900 Cummings Center, Suite 221
Beverly, MA 01915
aats.org

American Board of Medical
   Specialties
1007 Church Street, Suite 104
Evanston, IL 60201-5913
abms.org

American College of Cardiology
Heart House
9111 Old Georgetown Road
Bethesda, MD 20814-1699
acc.org

American College of Chest
   Physicians
3300 Dundee Boulevard
Northbrook, IL 60062-2348
chestnat.org

American College of Emergency
   Physicians
1125 Executive Circle
Irving, TX 75038-2522
acep.org

American College of
Gastroenterologists
P.O. Box 34220
Bethesda, MD 20827-2260
acg.gi.org

American College of Nuclear
Medicine
101 Broad Street
Philadelphia, PA 18201
acnumed.com

American College of Physicians
190 N. Independence Mall W.
Philadelphia, PA 19106-1572
acponline.org

American College of Preventive
Medicine
1307 New York Avenue NW
Washington, DC 20005
acpm.org

American College of Radiology
1899 Preston White Drive
Reston, VA 20191
acr.org

American College of Rheumatology
1800 Century Place, Suite 250
Atlanta, GA 30345-4300
rheumatology.org

American College of Surgeons
633 N. St. Clair Street
Chicago, IL 60611-3211
facs.org

American College Testing Program
500 ACT Drive
P.O. Box 188
Iowa City, IA 52243-0168
act.org

American Diabetes Association
1701 Beauregard Street
Alexandria, VA 22314-3357
diabetes.org

American Geriatrics Association
350 Fifth Avenue, Suite 801
New York, NY 10019
americangeriatrics.org

American Heart Association
7272 Greenville Avenue
Dallas, TX 75231
americanheart.org

American Lung Association
61 Broadway, 6th Floor
New York, NY 10006
lungusa.org

American Medical Association
515 N. State Street
Chicago, IL 60610-0174
ama-assn.org

American Medical College
Application Service (AMCAS)
Association of American Medical
Colleges (AAMC)
2450 N Street NW
Washington, DC 20037-1126
aamc.org/students/amcas

American Medical Group
   Association
1422 Duke Street
Alexandria, VA 22314-3430
amga.org

American Medical Student
   Association
1902 Association Drive
Reston, VA 20191
amsa.org

American Medical Women's
   Association
801 N. Fairfax Street, Suite 400
Alexandria, VA 22314
amwa-doc.org

American Orthopaedic Association
6300 N. River Road
Rosemont, IL 60018
aoassn.org

American Osteopathic Association
142 W. Ontario Street
Chicago, IL 60611
osteopathic.org

American Psychiatric Association
1000 Wilson Boulevard, Suite 1825
Arlington, VA 22209-3901
psych.org

American Society of
   Anesthesiologists
5200 Northwest Highway
Park Ridge, IL 60068-2513
asahq.org

American Society of Clinical
   Oncology
1900 Duke Street
Alexandria, VA 22314
asco.org

American Society for Clinical
   Pathology
210 W. Harrison Street
Chicago, IL 60612
ascp.org

American Society of Colon and
   Rectal Surgeons
85 W. Algonquin Road, Suite 550
Arlington Heights, IL 60005
fascrs.org

American Society of Hematology
1900 M Street NW, Suite 200
Washington, DC 20036
hematology.org

American Society of Nephrology
1725 I Street NW, Suite 510
Washington, DC 20006
asn-online.org

American Society of Plastic
   Surgeons
444 Algonquin Road
Arlington Heights, IL 60005
plasticsurgery.org

American Thoracic Society
61 Broadway
New York, NY 10006-2755
thoracic.org

American Urological Association
1000 Corporate Boulevard
Bethesda, MD 21090
auanet.org

The Association of Faculties of
 Medicine of Canada
774 Echo Drive
Ottawa, ON K13 5P2

Canadian Medical Association
P.O. Box CP8650
1867 Alta Vista Street
Ottawa, ON K16 346
cma.ca

College of American Pathologists
325 Waukegan Road
Deerfield, IL 60093-2750
cap.org

Council of Medical Specialty
 Societies
51 Sherwood Terrace, Suite M
Lake Bluff, IL 60044-2232
cmss.org

Endocrine Society
8401 Connecticut Avenue
Chevy Chase, MD 20815
endo-society.org

Federation of State Medical Boards
P.O. Box 619850
Dallas, TX 75261-9850
fsmb.org

Infectious Diseases Society of
 America
66 Canal Center Plaza, Suite 600
Alexandria, VA 22314
idsociety.org

International College of Surgeons
U.S. Section
1516 N. Lake Shore Drive
Chicago, IL 60610-1694
ficsonline.org

Medical College Admission Test
 (MCAT)
Association of American Medical
 Colleges
2450 N Street NW
Washington, DC 20037-1127
aamc.org

National Association of Medical
 Examiners
430 Pryor Street
Atlanta, GA 30312
thename.org

National Board of Medical
 Examiners
3750 Market Street
Philadelphia, PA 19104-3102
nbme.org

National Board of Osteopathic
 Medical Examiners
8765 W. Higgins Road, Suite 200
Chicago, IL 60631
nbome.org

National Institutes of Health
9000 Rockville Pike
Bethesda, MD 20892
nih.gov

National Medical Association
1012 Tenth Avenue NW
Washington, DC 20001
nmanet.org

National Resident Matching
    Program
2450 N Street NW
Washington, DC 20001
nrmp.org

Radiological Society of North
    America
820 Jorie Boulevard
Oak Brook, IL 60623-2251
rsna.org

Renal Physicians Association
1700 Rockville Pike
Rockville, MD 20852
renalmd.org

Society for Vascular Surgery
633 N. St. Clair Street, 24th Floor
Chicago, IL 60611
svs.vascularweb.org

Society of Critical Care Medicine
701 Lee Street, Suite 200
Des Plaines, IL 60016
sccm.org

Society of Nuclear Medicine
1850 Samuel Morse Drive
Reston, VA 20190-536
interactive.snm.org

Society of Thoracic Surgeons
633 N. St. Clair Street, Suite 2320
Chicago, IL 60611
sts.org

SPECIALTY BOARDS

The American Board of Allergy
    and Immunology
510 Walnut Street, Suite 1701
Philadelphia, PA 19106-3699
abai.org

The American Board of
    Anesthesiology
401 Lake Boone Trail, Suite 510
Raleigh, NC 27603-7506
theaba.org

The American Board of Colon and
    Rectal Surgery
20600 Eureka Road, Suite 600
Taylor, MI 48140
abcrs.org

The American Board of
    Dermatology
Henry Ford Health System
One Ford Place
Detroit, MI 48202-3450
abderm.org

American Board of Emergency
   Medicine
3000 Coolidge Road
East Lansing, MI 48825-6319
abem.org

American Board of Family
   Medicine
2228 Young Drive
Lexington, KY 40505-4294
theabfm.org

American Board of Internal
   Medicine
510 Walnut Street, Suite 1700
Philadelphia, PA 19106-3699
abim.org

American Board of Medical
   Genetics
9650 Rockville Pike
Bethesda, MD 20814-3998
abmg.org

American Board of Neurological
   Surgery
Smith Tower
6550 Fannin Street
Houston, TX 77030-2701
abns.org

American Board of Nuclear
   Medicine
900 Veteran Avenue, Room 13
Los Angeles, CA 90024-1786
abnm.org

American Board of Obstetrics and
   Gynecology
2915 Vine Street, Suite 300
Dallas, TX 75204
abog.org

American Board of Ophthalmology
111 Presidential Boulevard,
   Suite 241
Bala Cynwyd, PA 19004-1075
abop.org

American Board of Orthopaedic
   Surgery
400 Silver Cedar Court
Chapel Hill, NC 27514
abos.org

The American Board of
   Otolaryngology
3050 Post Oak Boulevard,
   Suite 1700
Houston, TX 77056
aboto.org

The American Board of Pathology
P.O. Box 25915
Tampa, FL 33622-5915
abpath.org

American Board of Pediatrics
111 Silver Creek Court
Chapel Hill, NC 27514
abp.org

American Board of Physical
   Medicine and Rehabilitation
21 First Street SW, Suite 674
Rochester, MN 55902-3092
abpmr.org

American Board of Plastic Surgery
Seven Penn Center, Suite 400
1635 Market Street
Philadelphia, PA 19103-2204
abplsurg.org

The American Board of Preventive
   Medicine
9950 W. Lawrence Avenue,
   Suite 106
Schiller Park, IL 60146
abprevmed.org

The American Board of Psychiatry
   and Neurology
500 Lake Cook Road, Suite 335
Deerfield, IL 60015-5249
abpn.org

The American Board of Radiology
5255 E. Williams Circle, Suite 3200
Tucson, AZ 85711
theabr.org

The American Board of Surgery
1617 John F. Kennedy Boulevard
Suite 860
Philadelphia, PA 19100
absurgery.org

American Board of Thoracic
   Surgery
633 N. St. Clair Street, Suite 2340
Chicago, IL 60611
abts.org

The American Board of Urology
2216 Ivy Road
Charlottesville, VA 22903
abu.org

APPENDIX C

BIBLIOGRAPHY

CAREERS IN MEDICINE

American College of Surgeons. *Socioeconomic FactBook for Surgery.* Chicago: American College of Surgeons, 2005.

Association of American Medical Colleges. Careers in Medicine website for students. aamc.org/students/cim.

Baker, L. C. "Differences in Earnings Between Male and Female Physicians." *New England Journal of Medicine* 334, no. 5 (1991): 960–4.

Barnes, Michael. *So You Want to Be a Doctor?* VHS. Boston: WGBH Educational Foundation and Princeton: Films for the Humanitarian Sciences, 2004.

Barnes, Michael. *Survivor M.D.* VHS. Boston: WGBH Educational Foundation, 2003.

Barnes, Michael. *Making of a Doctor.* VHS. Boston: WGBH Educational Foundation, 2005.

Barone, James E., and Michael Ivy. "Residential Work Hours: The Five Stages of Grief." *Academic Medicine* 79: 379–80.

Becoming an M.D. Chicago: American Medical Association, 2005.

Considering a Career in Medicine? Washington, D.C.: Association of American Colleges, 2005.

Bradbury, C. D., D. K. King, and R. G. Middleton. "Female Urologists: A Growing Population." *Journal of Urology* 157, no. 5 (May 1997): 1854–6.

Davis, W. K., C. Colon, et al. "Medical Career Choice, Current Status of Research Literature." *Teaching and Learning in Medicine* 2 (1990): 130–8.

Donaldson, Ronald M., Jr. *A Yale Guide to Careers in Medicine and the Health Professions.* New Haven, CT: Yale University Press, 2003.

Garibaldi, Richard A., C. Popkave, and W. Bylsma. "Career Plans for Trainees in Internal Medical Programs." *Academic Medicine* 80 (2005): 507–12.

Croasdale, Myrle. "Hospitalists: The Next Generation." *American Medical News*, May 23, 2005.

Medicine: A Chance to Make a Difference. Washington, D.C.: Association of American Medical Colleges, and Chicago: American Medical Association, 2004.

Medicine as a Career. Chicago: American Medical Association, Division of Undergraduate Education, 2003.

"Physicians." In *Occupational Outlook Handbook, 2004–2005.* Washington, D.C.: Bureau of Labor Statistics, 2004.

Wright, John W. "Doctors." In *The American Almanac of Jobs and Salaries.* New York: Harper Perennial, 2000.

CHOOSING A MEDICAL CAREER

American Medical Association. *Graduate Medical Education Directory 2005–2006.* Chicago: American Medical Association, 2005.

American Society for Investigative Pathology. *Pathology as a Career in Medicine.* Bethesda, MD: The Intersociety Committee on Pathology Information, Inc., 2005.

Choosing a Specialty. Chicago: American Medical Association, 2003.

Colon and Rectal Surgery. Palatine, IL: American Society of Colon and Rectal Surgeons. fascrs.org/index.cfm.

Council of Teaching Hospitals Directory. Washington, D.C.: Association of American Medical Colleges, 2005.

Freeman, Brian. *The Ultimate Guide to Choosing a Medical Specialty.* New York: McGraw-Hill, 2000.

Health Forum/American Hospital Association. *American Hospital Association Guide to the Health Care Field.* Chicago: American Hospital Association. 2005. ama-assn.org/ama/pub/category/2375.html.

Iserson, Kenneth. *Getting Into a Residency.* 2nd ed. Tucson, AZ: Galen Press, 2000.

Medical School Admission Requirements. Washington, D.C.: Association of American Medical Colleges, 2005.

NRMP Directory. Evanston, IL: National Residency Matching Program. 2005.

NRMP Results & Data 2005. Washington, D.C.: Association of American Medical Schools, 2005.

Pediatrics: What's It Really Like. Elk Grove Village, IL: The American Academy of Pediatrics, 2000.

Rowley, B. D., et al. "Selected Characteristics of Graduates." *Journal of the American Medical Association* 266, no. 7 (1991): 936.

Stilwell, Nancy A., Mollie M. Wallick, Sara E. Thal, and Joseph A. Burleson. "Myers-Briggs Type and Specialty Choice: A New Look at an Old Question." *Teaching and Learning in Medicine* 12 (2000): 14–20.

Taylor, Anita. *How to Choose a Medical Specialty.* Philadelphia: W. B. Saunders, 1993.

Transitional Year Program Directory. Washington, D.C.: Association for Hospital Medical Education, 2005. ahme.org/publications/transitional.html.

Vaidya, N. A., et al. "Relationship Between Specialty Choice and Medical Student Temperament and Character Assessment with Cloninger Inventory." *Teaching and Learning in Medicine* 16 (2004): 150–6.

Which Medical Specialty for You? Evanston, IL: American Board of Medical Specialties, 1995.

FINANCING A MEDICAL EDUCATION

Borzo, Greg. "Solo Practice: A Contrarian's View." *American Medical News,* July 24, 1995.

Buying and Selling a Medical Practice: A Valuation Guide. Chicago: American Medical Association, 2003.

The Debt Management Workbook. Washington, D.C.: U.S. Department of Health and Human Services, 2001.

Directory of Graduate Education Programs. Chicago: American Medical Association, 2005.

Federal Student Aid Fact Sheet. Washington, D.C.: Department of Education, Student Aid Information Office. fafsa.ed.gov.

Financial and Management Manual for U.S. Medical Students. Washington, D.C.: Association of American Medical Colleges, 1994.

Financial Planning and Debt Management for Health Professions. New York: National Medical Fellowships, Inc. nmfonline.org.

Financial Planning Guide for Medical Students in the U.S. Harrisburg, PA: Educational and Scientific Trust of the Pennsylvania Medical Society. pamedsoc.org.

Financing Medical Education. Boston: Boston University School of Medicine, 1993.

Financing Your Professional Education. New York: National Medical Fellowships, Inc. nmfonline.org.

Gonzalez, Martin L., and Puling Zhang, eds. *Socioeconomic Characteristics of Medical Practice 1997–1998.* Chicago: American Medical Association Center for Health Policy Research, 1998.

Medical RBRVS: Resource-Based Relative Value Scale. Chicago: American Medical Association, 2005.

Physician Characteristics and Distribution in the United States. Chicago: American Medical Association, 2006.

Schlachter, G. A., and David R. Weber. *Directory of Financial Aids for Women, 2005–2007.* El Dorado, CA: Reference Service Press, 2005.

Todd, James R. *Physician's Survival Guide: Legal Pitfalls and Solutions.* Chicago: American Medical Association, 1991.

MEDICAL SCHOOL

American Medical Association. *GMED Companion: An Insider's Guide to Selecting a Residency Program 2005–2006.* Chicago: American Medical Association, 2006.

American Medical Association. *Graduate Medical Education Directory 2005–2006.* Chicago: American Medical Association, 2005.

Krieger, Gary F. "Are We Choosing the Best Students for Medical School?" Chicago: *American Medical News*, October 3, 1994.

Lerner, M. *Medical School: The Interview and the Applicant.* Hauppauge, NY: Barrons Educational Series, Inc., 1977.

Lorin, Scott, John Heffner, and Carson Shannon. "Attitude and Perception of Internal Medicine Residents Regarding Pulmonary and Critical Care Subspecialty Training." *Chest* 127 (2005): 630–6.

MCAT Programs. Iowa City, IA: The American College Testing Program.

Meads, M. *Getting In: A Guide for Pre-Med Students.* Reston, VA: American Medical Student Association, Premedical Education Task Force, 1993.

"Medical School Residents Give Thumbs Up to 80 Hour Limit," *American Medical News*, September 12, 2005.

Moller, Meredith T., ed. *Medical School Admissions Requirements: United States and Canada 2006–2007.* Washington, D.C.: Association of American Medical Colleges, 2005.

Nash, Ira S., and Richard C. Pasternak. "Physician: Educate Thyself." *Journal of the American Medical Association* 273 (May 17, 1995): 1533–4.

Slomski, Anita J. "Will Medical Schools Solve the Primary Care Shortage?" *Medical Economics* 70 (July 26, 1993): 87–99.

MEDICINE AS A PROFESSION

AAMC Data Book. Washington, D.C.: Association of American Medical Colleges, 2005.

Accreditation of Graduate Medical Education Programs. Chicago: Accreditation Council for Graduate Medical Education, 2005.

American College of Surgeons. "So, You Want to Be a Surgeon: A Medical Student's Online Guide to Finding and Matching with the Best Possible Surgical Residency." facs.org/residencysearch.

Becoming an M.D. Chicago: American Medical Association, 2005.

Cohen, Jordan M. *What to Be When You Grow Up.* Washington, D.C.: Association of American Medical Colleges, 2005.

Medical Specialty Certification and Related Matters. Washington, D.C.: Association of American Medical Colleges, 2005.

The Official ABMS Directory of Board Specialized Medical Specialists. Evanston, IL: American Board of Medical Specialties, 2005.

Pasko, Thomas, and Derek R. Smart. *Physician Characteristics and Distribution in the U.S.* Chicago: American Medical Association, 2005.

Physician Compensation in Specialty and Production Survey. Englewood, CO: Medical Group Management Association, 1995.

Physician Socioeconomic Statistics. Chicago: American Medical Association, 2005.

The Surgical Career Handbook. Chicago: American College of Surgeons, 2005.

OSTEOPATHY AS A CAREER

2004 American Osteopathic Association Directory. Chicago: American Osteopathic Association, 2004.

Osteopathic Medicine: A Distinctive Branch of Mainstream Medicine. Chicago: American Osteopathic Association, 2000.

Trends in Specialization: Tomorrow's Medicine. Evanston, IL: American Board of Medical Specialties, 2000.

What Everyone Should Know About Osteopathic Medicine. Chicago: American Osteopathic Association, 2001.

What Is a D.O.? What Is an M.D.? Chicago: American Osteopathic Association, 2003.

MINORITIES IN MEDICINE

Financial Management for Minorities in Medical Fields. Garrett Park, MD: Garrett Park Press, 1996.

Health Pathways. 19th ed. Sacramento, CA: Health Professions Career Opportunity Program, 1999.

Krapp, Kristine. *Notable Black American Scientists.* Detroit: Gale, 1999.

Minorities in Medical Education: Facts and Figures, 2005. Washington, D.C.: Association of American Medical Colleges, 2005.

Minorities in Medicine: Health Professions Opportunities for Minorities. Sacramento, CA: Office of Statewide Health Planning and Development, Health Professions Center Opportunities Program, 1999.

Schlachter, G. A., and D. Weber. *Directory of Financial Aid for Minorities.* San Carlos, CA: Reference Service Press, 2005.

Bickel, Jan. "Women in Academic Medicine." *Journal of the American Medical Women's Association* 55, no. 1 (2000): 10–12.

Clapp, Patricia. *Dr. Elizabeth Blackwell: A Biography of the First Woman Doctor.* New York: Lathrop, Lee & Shepard, 2004.

Garza, Hedda. *Women in Medicine.* New York: Franklin Watts, 1994.

Kaplan, S. "Motivation for Women Over 30 Going into Medical School." *Journal of Medical Education* 56, no. 10 (1981): 856–8.

Kerkstein, R. L. "Women Physicians—Good News and Bad" *New England Journal of Medicine* 334, no. 15 (April 11, 1996): 982–3.

Klass, Perry. *A Not Entirely Benign Procedure: Four Years as Medical Student.* New York: G. P. Putnam, 1997.

Lillemoe, K., et al. "Surgery—Still an Old Boys Club?" *Surgery* 116 (1994): 255–61.

Mendelsohn, K., et al. "Sex and Gender Bias in Anatomy and Physical Diagnosis." *Journal of the American Medical Association* 272 (1994): 1267–70.

Nonnamaker, Lynn. "Women Physicians in Academic Medicine." *New England Journal of Medicine* 342, no. 6 (2000): 982–3.

Walters, Beverly C., and Irene Y. McNeil. *The Annotated Bibliography of Women in Medicine.* Ontario, Canada: Ontario Medical Association, 1993.

ABOUT
THE AUTHOR

Terry Sacks is an independent writer-editor with more than thirty years' experience in communications. During that period he has written dozens of news stories, magazine articles, and speeches. Sacks's articles have appeared in such publications as *Hospitals*, *The Kiwanis Magazine*, and *Chicago Medicine*.

Sacks, a graduate of Northwestern's Medill School of Journalism, has strong credentials in the health-care field. For three years, from 1970 through 1973, he was director of communications for the Chicago Medical Society, the local professional group for physicians in Chicago and Cook County. He has in addition held positions in communications for the American Association of Dental Schools and for several hospitals in Chicago.

Sacks was formerly on the journalism faculty at Columbia College in Chicago, where in addition to teaching Introduction of the Mass Media he has taught courses in news reporting, feature writing, editing company publications, and the history of journalism.

For the past fifteen years, Sacks has headed his own writing and communications firm, Terence J. Sacks Associates. He is active in the Independent Writers of Chicago, the American Medical Writers Association, and the Publicity Club of Chicago.

His daughter, Lili, an internist who practices in Seattle, Washington, has been most helpful in the completion of this manuscript.